WHAT A CEO CAN LEARN
From a 4th Grader

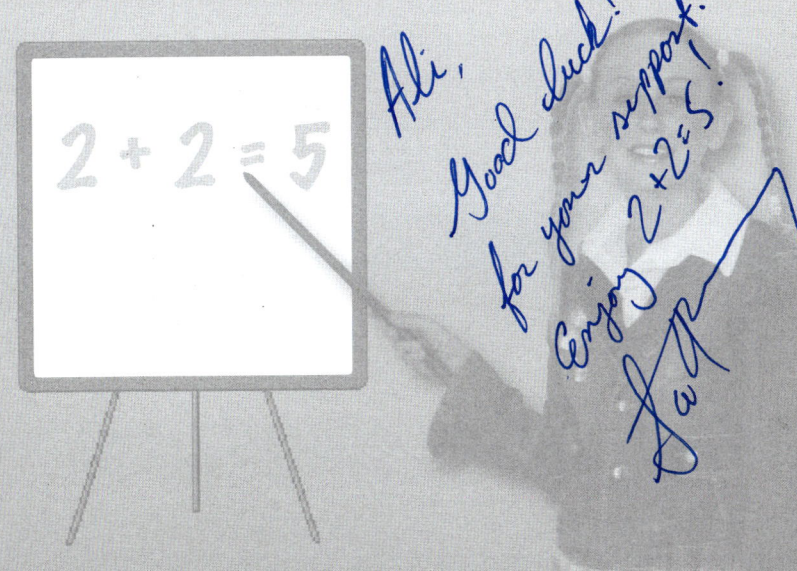

2 + 2 = 5

Ali,
Good luck! Thanks
for your support.
Enjoy 2+2=5!

SCOTT P. MORENCY

TABLE OF CONTENTS

Acknowledgements 5

Dedication 7

Preface 9

Introduction 13

Chapter One:
Emotional Intelligence 25

Chapter Two:
Team Trust 49

Chapter Three:
Clear and Effective Communication 69

Chapter Four:
Leadership 87

Chapter Five:
Essential Diversity 101

Chapter Six:
Problem Solving 117

Chapter Seven:
Negotiation 131

Conclusion 145

ACKNOWLEDGMENTS

The author wishes to acknowledge those that have been absolutely instrumental in his success with the 2+2=5 program and in support of the writing of *What a CEO can learn from a 4th Grader* and in the development of the 2+2=5 program. The author acknowledges that life's greatest successes are engineered by successful teams and Scott would like to extend appreciation to his team:

To the Bentley Service-Learning Center for their support with the 2+2=5 program, without which the program would never have grown its wings. In particular, the author recognizes the love and support from the staff: Jeannette MacInnes, Lynne Johanson, Shawn Hauserman, and Franklyn Salimbene.

To the all-star student and faculty cast that helped to develop, manage, and refine the 2+2=5 program with their commitment to continual growth. Special thanks extended to Manny Carneiro, Danielle Boczar, Aaron Nurick, and Angelique Davi for helping to push the 2+2=5 program to unimaginable heights.

To the elementary schools of Waltham, Massachusetts for recognizing the need for interpersonal skill development in our young children. 2+2=5 will always find its foundation in Waltham elementary schools. Special recognition for the vision and support of school adminis-

ACKNOWLEDGEMENTS

trators Alice Shull and Diane Fischer. To the Waltham elementary school students who taught me so much about teamwork through their actions and words.

To the two most important women in my life: Laura Doane for your love and unwavering support of my work and to my mother, Diane Griffin, for always lending an ear of support and words of encouragement. Without the help of family, this work would simply not be possible. Additionally, Scott extends special thanks for the unending support and encouragement from his best friend and brother, Craig Morency.

Finally, Scott wants to take the opportunity to recognize that all good things come from God; Scott would like to take a moment to praise and glorify God for His work, evident in the 2+2=5 program.

Dedication

The 2+2=5 program was created in 2003, but the seeds were planted years and years before. When a plant comes to growth, it's essential to recognize the work of the gardener. For all of his wisdom, guidance, love, and most of all, for the seeds that he planted in my spirit, I dedicate this work to my father, Paul Morency, the finest teacher of life's little lessons.

Preface

2+2=5: The Power of Teamwork, is an intensive teambuilding program that leverages teambuilding activities through the use of reflection to discover, develop, and enhance interpersonal skills such as leadership, communication, diversity on teams, trust, problem solving, negotiation, and emotional intelligence. The 2+2=5 program was created in 2003 in Waltham, Massachusetts.

The 2+2=5 program provides university students the opportunity to serve in the community as a mentor and team coach for the participating children. The program was originally designed for fourth and fifth grade elementary students, and to be led and facilitated by university students. The coach facilitates teambuilding activities in which the children focus on the development of interpersonal skills. The facilitator uses team reflections to leverage learning opportunities. The 2+2=5 program is currently being expanded to include corporate teambuilding.

The results of the 2+2=5 program have been presented at conferences across the country and for the first time are being shared in this book. The 2+2=5 program has since further grown, being adopted both across the United States and internationally. 2+2=5 has even been expanded to corporate teambuilding focusing on the professional development of employees and developing a team dynamic in workplace culture.

When the 2+2=5 program was first created, I thought we, as college business students, would have the

PREFACE

opportunity to teach a bunch of children about teamwork. What I didn't expect when I first set out is that the children taught me as much as I taught them, which became the foundation of *What a CEO can Learn from a 4th Grader.*

Some reactions to the 2+2=5 program:

"Two plus two really *does* equal five. The games we play really teach us that teamwork is important. For most of these games, we couldn't accomplish the goal, unless we worked as a team," said Ashley, fourth grade student.

"I never really realized that we use teamwork everyday! It takes a lot of hard work to develop a team, but once we did, we really saw results," stated Christopher, fifth grade student.

"I can't believe how much I learned from the program. I thought I knew everything there was to know about leadership until I saw the activities in motion. It shed new light on what I thought I already knew," added Marcus, college junior student.

"2+2=5 really challenges you to think more deeply about the way we interact as teams. I never thought about how dynamic teams really can be. I'm sure that my experience in this program will be useful when I graduate," said Stephanie, college sophomore student.

The 2+2=5 program has had over 3,000 children and 500 college students go through the program and each participant has taken a unique experience from 2+2=5. We have seen ten and eleven year-old children thrive in a team atmosphere quickly being able to pick up team skills, applying it to an activity, and even teaching us a thing or two in the process.

We have even seen *life-changing* moments. So often, the words "life-changing" are used that they take on form of a hyperbole, but in some cases, the 2+2=5 program has been, without a doubt, life-changing.

Take Jenny, for example, a selective mute, unable and unwilling to speak to adults who, through 2+2=5, was able to break out of her troubling disorder and flourish as a leader on her team. Please see the leadership chapter for Jenny's remarkable story.

2+2=5 is a complex idea and built through the use of interpersonal building blocks, but it's not so complex in the eyes of a child. It's amazing who we can learn from if we open our eyes and ears. Come along for a journey as the teacher becomes the student. This is what I learned from some fourth and fifth graders…

INTRODUCTION

Teamwork and collaboration are skills and qualities that many managers would describe as a relatively easy concept to understand, but not easily put into practice effectively. It is this disconnect between conceptualizing the idea of teamwork and actually putting it into practice that leads to the frustration of managers. This social disconnect also leads to unquantifiable hours lost and dollars spent because of inefficient production and strained working relationships.

One of the most common complaints of business managers today is that employees do not work well together in teams within the workplace environment. When it comes to team skills, most people are able to talk a good game. For example, teamwork is something just about anyone will mention in an interview, "I would say that my biggest strength would be that I am a team player." However, on day one of employment with the company, that same person is willing to compromise these team values in order to get ahead.

Teamwork and interpersonal skills are something that everyone can talk about on a job interview, in a board meeting, on the baseball diamond, or in a classroom, but while the nature of these skills seems simple in concept, they are extraordinarily more difficult in practice. Team skills seem difficult in practice based on the fact that they are overwhelmingly absent from many corporate environments. In fact, without much struggle, it is easy for most people to think of a moment when teamwork was missing from their own workplace.

Case in point: Imagine you are an advertising account representative for a well known newspaper. Each month, you have an ad sales quota of $10,000. Not only is each sales representative expected to meet the quota each month and there are additional incentives for the top sales representative each month. On the 29th of the month, you have met your quota with sales of $12,500. You are the leading salesperson for the month with the second place salesperson, Bob, trailing with $12,250. At your morning coffee break, you notice an incoming fax addressed to Bob with an ad request from a new client that would put Bob in the lead for ad sales with only one day left in the month. With a $1,000 incentive bonus looming, you decide that you will hold onto the fax until after the first of the month in order to secure the bonus. You win the bonus; three days later you put the fax on Bob's desk. Excited for the lead, Bob calls the potential client and discovers that due to the delay, they had already placed their new ad with a competing newspaper.

The company loses potentially hundreds of thousands of dollars in future business. Who is ultimately at fault? While you have certainly acted unethically, the blame extends further. There are so many reasons why teamwork is missing in the office. One of those reasons relates to the way we are evaluated for compensation or promotions being based on individual accomplishment. Too often today, compensation and evaluation programs discourage the development of highly effective teams in work environments.

The way that employees interact with each other is largely a product of the tone at the top from management. The concept of the tone at the top suggests that the behaviors and attitudes of management will ultimately ripple, being reflected in the employees of the company. It is management's responsibility to set the tone and develop a fertile ground for team development. Managers, who fail to create a culture where teamwork and collaboration is cultivated and rewarded, fall victim to destructive employees who are only aligning their behavior with the reward structure and tone at the top established by management.

People, as it seems, are perfectly willing to take part in the nature of cutthroat tactics in order to further their personal success and climb up along the corporate ladder, especially where management has established a tone at the top that rewards this behavior. Employees must put themselves first, no matter the cost to their co-workers, even if it means sacrificing the success and profitability of the business for which they are employed. Management puts in place these incentives for individual achievement as a basis for improving overall company performance. What they may not realize is that these incentive structures detract from the success that teamwork and team synergy can bring.

Indeed, there are multiple causes and triggers for the lack of teamwork displayed in the workplace. Whether it is due to poorly constructed incentive programs, management's tone at the top or just a lack of skill development opportunities for employees, a lack of teamwork is a predominant problem in the workplace.

First, managers must be convinced of the benefit of teamwork in the workplace. Then, they must recognize the lack of teamwork as a problem. Finally, managers must be willing to devote the resources necessary to foster a team environment.

The lack of ability to work well in teams, however, does not stop in the workplace. It seems to be missing even from family life. Stunning statistics seem to show nearly a fifty percent divorce rate in the United States in recent years.[1] Without a doubt, our family is very much a team and unless families work and play as a team, families will continue to splinter. We have seen an absence of teamwork in the workplace but why are we seeing similar trends in our personal lives?

One way involves the introduction of new technologies. As much as technology has advanced our society for recent decades, it has not come without some negative impact. From our working relationships to our personal friendships, the impact of technology advancements has reared its ugly head against interpersonal development and eliminating our ability to develop these interpersonal skills.

Imagine you are a new hire at a financial services firm. You are working on a team sitting in individual office cubes. You have a question for another team member who is sitting in the cube next to you. Instead of standing up and walking to that team member's cube, you send them an instant message or an email. These technology

---

[1] According to a compilation of research from http://divorcerate.org

advances actually serve as barriers to interpersonal development. People are relying more on instant messaging, emailing, and text messaging than picking up the phone or making a personal face to face visit. How can someone develop and refine their interpersonal skill set without actually interacting with others on a face to face basis?

Recognizing a lack of teamwork as a problem is only half the battle. What is the solution to this overwhelming societal problem? In order reverse this problem, it is essential to identify from where it originates. The question is, in fact, where does this problem seem to begin?

First and foremost, the problem originates with the development of our children. The foundation and basis for interpersonal development begins in childhood. Where do children learn about teambuilding, collaboration, effective communication, leadership skills and how to use and apply these skills? The answer seems to be that children are left to learn about these interpersonal skills mostly on their own, based on what they witness from their parents and other adults or based on how they interact with their peers. Children learn these skills without any real opportunity for refinement. Despite the fact that these interpersonal skills have become increasingly recognized as a critical set of life skills, we simply do not devote the resources necessary to teach our children about teamwork.

Certainly there are some limited channels for children to learn teamwork, such as through scouting, school student councils, and after-school programs for example. Arguably, these interpersonal skills are also pseudo-represented in some youth sports. But it can be argued that these skills are often even torn down in youth sports. How often have we opened the newspaper to find out that another fight has broken out at a hockey game between a father and his son's coach for lack of playing time for his son? Or who can argue that we have seen parents live through their child's individual accomplishment, with the parents emphasizing individual accomplishment over the success of the team? Opportunities for children to learn teambuilding skills is vanishing from popular culture; subsequently impacting work environments and families everywhere as children grow older.

If children don't have the opportunity to learn these skills in the traditional environments in the way that we would think, then where are they learned? Do you think that these skills are taught in elementary education? President Bush's *No Child Left Behind Act* dramatically shifted the focus within the classroom. The positive or negative impact of this act is truly beyond the scope and the goals of this book; however, surely both supporters and opponents of the *No Child Left Behind Act* would admit that the landscape of the elementary classroom has shifted dramatically, requiring teachers to specifically hit key learning points in each school year that will be covered on a standardized state exam. This emphasis of "teaching to the test" leaves little time for classroom development of interpersonal or team skills as teachers struggle to cover required material. This ultimately results in the closing of an enormous opportunity for our children to develop these skills in the classroom at a young age. Teachers simply do not have enough of the finite resource of time to properly emphasize the development of these critical life skills.

In response to the observed deficiency in children's education and interpersonal skill development, 2+2=5 The Power of Teamwork was developed at Bentley College in Waltham, Massachusetts through the Bentley Service-Learning Center. The 2+2=5 program was designed to directly address the need for interpersonal skills development in elementary education. The goal was to better understand how elementary students would react to an opportunity to build and develop these interpersonal skills as well as discuss the relevance to teams and team success. The program is called '2+2=5, The Power of Teamwork' inferring that people can accomplish more by working together than by concentrating on individual accomplishment.

Essentially, 2+2=5 means that when teamwork is employed, "the whole is greater than the sum of all parts." 2+2=5 has been primarily designed for college business students to have the opportunity to perform community service in local elementary schools. 2+2=5 was adopted by elementary schools in the northeast, in particular for fourth and fifth grade elementary students in an effort to teach and instruct the students on many different fronts relating to personal growth. 2+2=5 was created with the vision that while the concept of teams, the importance of teamwork, and the understanding of critical interpersonal skills have been somewhat lost in today's youth, it is critical to first develop and then sub-

INTRODUCTION

sequently reinforce those concepts in the classroom in an environment built around peers, teachers, and mentors.

Fundamentally, the program instructs, through regular weekly sessions, the participating elementary students to become better team players, to enhance and build leadership skills, to understand team empowerment. In addition the program focuses on the ability to comprehend the different roles that team members serve, to build communication skills such as active listening and non-verbal communication, to enrich interpersonal relations, to understand conflict resolution and the benefits of constructive conflict. Finally, the program as seeks to develop intuitive problem solving skills, to build trust in themselves and their teammates, to learn the difference between a group and a team as well as the stages a group goes through to become a team and to understand the concept of emotional intelligence.

All of these personal and professional skills are inarguably critical for success in all aspects of life and are not currently being developed in an elementary school setting. The 2+2=5 program was designed to build and develop these skills with the students through team building and problem solving activities and exercises. Each exercise is led by a college student mentor and is followed with a reflection of that exercise to assure that the students were relating the activity to one of the skills that is being developed. This book includes several of the 2+2=5 activities. The instructions and reflection questions have been modified to be more appropriate for an audience of professionals.

In addition, the program was designed such that the students would have a chance to be exposed to each isolated skill set twice and in two different learning environments. The sessions completed have been in conjunction with the students' drama and physical education classes. Each week, the students will begin by learning about a topic such as emotional intelligence in their drama classes and work on an activity or game that was designed primarily for a classroom atmosphere about the topic. Following the drama class session, the students will then have a follow-up session, later in the week, with college student facilitators in their physical education class.

Each week, the targeted skill also requires the use of the interpersonal building block lessons developed from previous weeks. The designated activities require that all skills that have been previously taught in the program would be necessary for success. In other words, the activities build upon each other in every successive week. For instance, the first session introduces the topic of teams in distinction from groups and how groups become teams. The following weeks involve topics such as communication, problem solving, roles in teams, leadership, trust, and emotional intelligence. This gives the facilitators an opportunity to reinforce each skill that has been developed during each successive week, in an attempt to continually further develop and refine the skills that had been developed in previous weeks through the program. The 2+2=5 program attempts to develop these skills like building blocks, first establishing a foundation and then continuing to refine the skills.

INTRODUCTION

2+2=5 has provided an incredible opportunity to assess how the classes of elementary students learn, adapt, develop, react, and refine critical interpersonal skills. Each session requires the elementary school students to reflect upon the activity completed. The facilitator poses reflection questions. The students' responses are diligently recorded to track the progress of the students.

When first developing the 2+2=5 program, I thought that this was an opportunity for me was to teach children these team skills; I never expected how much I would learn from the children. In fact, I would argue that the children taught me more about teamwork than I ever taught them. The children taught me about teamwork and leadership, boiling down complex ideas with simple words and actions, through the eyes of ten year-olds.

The 2+2=5 program not only measures the results of the children participants but also records the development and learning of the college student facilitators. One way in which the 2+2=5 program measured the college students' learning is through the use of reflection journals. Each college student facilitator has been required to maintain a learning journal to share what they have learned from the 2+2=5 experience.

As business school students, particularly management students, the facilitators, at first, seemed to be the perfect experts on the subject of interpersonal and team skills. Through journal sharing and discussions, it was discovered that the college students were learning as much, if not more, from the children's learning, than they had ever imagined possible. The children often had a very intuitive, lucid, and creative way of sharing their thoughts on several critical interpersonal and team skills. The 2+2=5 program provided a myriad of opportunities for the college business students to learn from the young children's perspective on teamwork.

After identifying a lack of effective teamwork and collaboration in many work environments, it became clear that the fourth and fifth graders in the 2+2=5 program might have a few things to teach CEOs and other managers. And so this book is designed to share children's wisdom on critical topics such as emotional intelligence, trust, leadership, communication, problem solving, negotiation, and diversity. Children have the unique ability to put things in a different perspective, often both simple and complex at the same time. The perspective that children can offer in understanding the development of these skills is invaluable.

In addition, each section of this book provides examples of some of the teambuilding activities in which the children participate in with the 2+2=5 program. Managers and team leaders can use these activities to exercise team building skills in their teams. The activities include a series of reflection questions that are designed to facilitate reflective discussion. The key to leveraging these activities as a learning opportunity is using reflective discussion. The reflection questions have been slightly modified to more appropriately facilitate reflection and discussion for a more mature, professional audience. Facilitators of the activities are primarily responsible for critically observing the activity and taking notice of the

INTRODUCTION

way in which the team functions throughout the activity. The facilitator can modify the reflection questions to specifically address observations from the activities. While these activities are part of the 2+2=5 program, they are only a sampling of the original program.

Managers can facilitate these activities in order to help develop these qualities and skills in their employees and build a culture where teamwork and collaboration is encouraged and fostered. Managers must set the "tone at the top", building an environment where teamwork is rewarded. This book explores the way in which the children have approached the 2+2=5 activities and what they have taught business students over the last several years. Perhaps, professional managers, business owners, and CEOs can learn a little from some ten and eleven year-old consultants!

The setup of this book is such that each chapter isolates a skill that is essential for team success. Each chapter begins by setting the table for the need for each skill in the workplace by describing a workplace situation where that particular skill would have been useful. Then each chapter contains a couple of the 2+2=5 activities and reflections that are designed to develop that particular skill. Managers may consider facilitating these activities with their work teams as an opportunity to exercise and develop team skills. The remainders of each chapter shares stories and quotes from fourth and fifth grade children that detail what the children have taught the college business students.

CHAPTER ONE

EMOTIONAL INTELLIGENCE

"Emotions are Contagious" – Christina, fourth grade

A Day in the Office

The March 31st deadline is looming eerily close. The project has been progressing well but there have been some unexpected bumps in the road. Charlene, the manager, knows the difficult news she must deliver to the team: it's going to be several late nights for the next two weeks until the project deadline. Charlene carefully crafts how to deliver the tough news to the team, trying to put a positive spin on the situation. The team's morning smile quickly melted to a depressed, disgusted attitude. Charlene knew she had one hope, Marco.

Marco has always been the lifeline of the project team. He's always upbeat even in the most stress laden and down trodden times. The team could hardly go a day without seeing his smiling face or laughing at one of his lighthearted jokes. When Marco heard the news, he took it in stride and smiled, cracking another joke. Immediately the team's mood shifted. The positive attitude Marco carried, almost instantly spreading to the rest of the team.

Then in walked Nellie. She was always complaining. In fact, no one ever wanted to work with her be-

EMOTIONAL INTELLIGENCE

cause all she would do is complain about anything and everything. When she heard the news, Nellie's attitude got even worse. Whenever the manager, Charlene, got up from the workroom, Nellie would talk bad about Charlene, complaining about her poor management. When Nellie went to get coffee in the break room, she saw another team member and started complaining again about the long work hours and how terrible this job was. This quickly became reflected in the second employee and before long the negative attitude had once again resurfaced on the team. Gradually, each team member began to share Nellie's negative attitude.

Emotions are often triggered by both events and occurrences and the people by which we are surrounded. Whether your team has a Marco or a Nellie, or both, emotions are contagious, period. The challenge for any manager is how to manage emotions and leverage positive emotions to improve the team's effectiveness and efficiency. This chapter focuses on emotional intelligence and the way in which we manage and leverage emotions, essential for teams.

Many managers often think of emotional intelligence or emotional management as a "soft" part of the job that is extraneous to the main responsibility of the job: managing a project. If managers think of their job as managing people as opposed to managing projects then emotional management takes center stage. Emotions must not only be managed but can also be leveraged to enhance the team output. Emotional intelligence can be developed with use of the following 2+2=5 activities:

Straw Skyscraper Activity

Each team is to receive twenty five drinking straws, five feet of scotch tape or masking tape and twenty five small paper clips. All teams begin together and have twenty minutes to construct the tallest skyscraper out of the materials provided to each team. Of course, facilitators have the ability to manipulate the variables, such as how many straws or how much time to complete the project. These variables are dependent upon time, resources, and management's goals for the activity.

The structures must be completely freestanding and cannot be adhered to the floor or ceiling. The team with the tallest structure at the end of the activity is the winner. Careful attention must be paid to the process employed by the team, taking into consideration the extent of the planning and strategy development, as well as a team's willingness to stop construction in favor of committing time to evaluate and assess its strategy.

Reflection Questions: Please note that the following questions can be used by the facilitator to help lead the reflection discussion after the activity is completed. Facilitators can use these questions or other questions generated as a result of the observations from the activity.

- Describe the process that which your team used to complete this activity. Was it effective? Upon reflection, how could your team's approach have been more successful?

EMOTIONAL INTELLIGENCE

- What interpersonal skills were important in this activity? What did we learn about those skills that we can use in our everyday life?
- What are some effective ways for teams to develop strategies? Are these consistent with what you use in other team activities?
- How did small successes or small setbacks during the activity impact the morale and emotions of the team? Were emotions contagious between individuals on the team?
- How did the contagious emotions affect the team? What can we learn about the importance of team morale for ourselves and others?

WHAT A CEO CAN LEARN FROM A 4th GRADER

Radio Activity

The facilitator will arrange one setup for each team. Using masking tape or rope, the facilitator will mark off a circle on the floor of about ten feet in diameter. In the middle of the circle place two bowls: one empty and one full of paper clips (or some other substance of similar weight. Outside of the circle, place 4 six foot length ropes and two rubber bands.

The facilitator directs the teams by reading the following excerpt: "There has been a radioactive spill on the floor and the circle represents the extent of the toxic area. The radio active waste is contained in the bowl in the middle of the circle, represented by the bowl with paper clips. However, the existing bowl is cracked and its contents must be transferred to the empty bowl within the circle. The bowls must not be slid across the floor and no team member may cross into or lean over the toxic area. The first team to successfully complete the transfer of the radioactive waste is the winner."

Facilitator note: (Solution) The team must tie one end of each individual rope to the rubber band. Each team member stands evenly spread around the circle, each holding one end of a rope, leave the rubber band central to the "lifting contraption". The team members gently pull on their ropes, sufficiently stretching the rubber band over the top of the bowl. Once the rubber band surrounds the bowl, the team releases the pressure, allowing the band to tighten around the bowl. The team

EMOTIONAL INTELLIGENCE

lifts the bowl together and carefully transfers the contents to the second bowl.

Reflection Questions: Please note that the following questions can be used by the facilitator to help lead the reflection discussion after the activity is completed. Facilitators can use these questions or other questions generated as a result of the observations from the activity.

- How did your team approach the activity? What methods did your team use that seemed more effective? What could you have done differently?
- If your team was not the first to complete the activity, how did the increased pressure impact the team dynamic?
- What emotions were expressed by members of your team? How did the emotions impact the performance during the activity? How do the emotions of others impact our performance with other tasks?
- What is the team leader's responsibility with regard to channeling positive emotion?

WHAT A CEO CAN LEARN FROM A 4th GRADER

Emotional Intelligence

Begin by taking a slice of elementary school life in Anytown, USA:

Another fight has broken out on the school playground at recess today between Billy and Joey. It's hard to understand what exactly happened as the students, now separated, both belt out different stories through the tears that inhibit their speech and concentration. All you know is that you heard voices escalate to a scream, each bit of anger building onto the accumulated mass of emotional tension. Billy and Joey have been emotionally hijacked.[2]

Johnny has been withdrawn from his classes all day. It's clear to the teacher that something is bothering him but he won't say what. When asked, he insists that nothing is wrong, choosing to bottle up his emotion. What his teacher does not know is that Johnny's family pet is being put to sleep this afternoon. Johnny has been emotionally hijacked.

Tina and Jenny sit at the lunch room table bickering about whether or not Tina had a crush on Matt. Tina's clearly embarrassed, red face signals that she had enough of this argument. She picks up her end of the table sending four cafeteria trays of food falling back onto Jenny. Jenny stands quickly, but she's too late, completely covered in Jell-O and pudding and crying uncontrollably. Tina and Jenny have been emotionally hijacked.

---

[2] The term "emotional hijacking" as used by Daniel Goleman in *Working with Emotional Intelligence*

EMOTIONAL INTELLIGENCE

Becoming emotionally hijacked typically occurs when the emotional state that we are in controls our behaviors and our actions. These emotional hijackings are by no means limited to ten year-olds. Imagine your coworkers:

Roberto is at the photo copier, beating his fists against the sides of the copier trying to unjam the paper tray. Roberto is emotionally hijacked. Imagine Suzie, missing her afternoon appointments because she has just gotten an email from her husband about last night's fight. Suzie is emotionally hijacked. Imagine Ramon fading from his tasks; he just received a bonus and is already thinking about the new pool he is going to put in. Ramon is emotionally hijacked.

It is quite more than an oversight that there is such little emphasis or understanding of the role that emotion plays in the way that we function in everyday life. Without a doubt, however, all of those emotionally stirring scenarios have happened in some school or some workplace, somewhere at some time and likely not that long ago. Something like this is probably happening in your organization everyday. It is likely that we all are overtaken by our emotions at some point each day; what matters most is how we understand and manage these emotions. Everyone has a distinct set of emotions and not nearly enough emphasis is placed on the importance of understanding emotional intelligence, both in businesses and even through the eyes of elementary student children.

Quite certainly the term 'emotional intelligence' has become a hot-button in corporate environments lately and in American popular culture. It is increasingly evident that our emotions are developed in the early stages of our lives. The temperament that we develop early on plays a significant role in our emotional make-up throughout our lives. Therefore, more attention should be placed on the emotions that children feel, how they affect their daily experiences, and how they may affect other students. Emotions are contagious. We do not live in a vacuum. Children are easily, emotionally affected, therefore pronouncing the contagiousness of emotions even more clearly. Emotional intelligence is critical to the success of every team and each individual personally particularly because of the ease in transference of contagious emotions.

Conveyance of Emotion

Emotions are conveyed in many different ways, most of which we are not primarily conscious of when we are conveying them. Most people think that emotions are conveyed through verbally telling and other forms of verbal communication. Discussing emotions with a friend or confidant is only one simple method in which emotion is conveyed between people.

A smile, a sigh, rolling of eyes, wrinkled eye brow, a stare, crossing of arms, a tear, a scream, a moan, a laugh, a nod, a shake, a frown: these emotions are displayed during practically every moment of each day. We communicate our emotions to others in a variety of different ways whether we are aware of it or not. The fourth grade children certainly demonstrated and provided evidence suggests the power of emotions in the way that we communicate. Understanding that emotion plays a critical role in communication suggests that managers can use this information to become more effective communicators. Understanding emotion and the importance of empathy is a critical component of successful and effective communication.

Words and sounds are the primary way in which we think and expect emotions to be conveyed. Indeed, in several challenging team activities, students expressed frustration and discouragement both verbally and nonverbally, "What's the point of this stupid game anyway? We'll never get it?" one student always said. Other members of his team, clearly frustrated with him, would moan or groan heavily to signify their frustration which was as evident as the explicit student in many of the activities.

During several activities, after a briefing on the importance of self-awareness to individuals and teams, we would frequently stop and ask individuals to talk about what they were feeling at that particular freeze in the game. The activity that we selected for the week involved an incredibly difficult task that would require the entire class to work exceptionally well together or else it would certainly fail. Unfortunately, within the time constraints, the class was not able to complete the task given to them. I intentionally gave them a shortened period of time to complete the activity and frequently reminded them of their shortage of time and how little they had left in order to invoke frustration and to see how the students would respond. One student, responsible for holding the rope in which the team was required cross, repeatedly breached the rules by lowering the rope and causing his team to have to start over.

Naturally, the class became increasingly frustrated with him and made it well known to him. Finally, the pressure had reached its peak and the student rope holder threw the rope down in disgust, kicking it aside and storming to the back wall of the gym. Within seconds, I summoned him back to the group to discuss his emotions. We talked about how he had displayed his emotions without even saying a word or mumbling anything.

The class came to the ultimate conclusion that when looking for the right signals, it is quite easy to understand the emotions of others without the subject even saying a word. Emotions are conveyed in many different ways, facial expressions, tone, gestures, actions, and of course in words. We often express our emotions without even being conscious of doing so. When asked what does it mean to "express your emotions" one male student responded, "Talk about your feelings and stupid stuff like that… like girls do." Ironically, it was the same student that had so clearly expressed his emotions - - - frustration and anger with the rope, only thirty minutes earlier.

Certainly, not all experiences stir up emotions in similar ways. There are several events and experiences throughout the duration of the program that have proven that teams go through several emotional processes, especially dynamic teams of children during activities that are exciting and frustrating at times.

One of those team processes involves the process of choosing a leader, which the teams frequently were required to do in a strict time constraint. During the first attempt at choosing a leader, the teams attempted to choose an emotionless random process by choosing a leader through some method of random selection. At which point, I stopped the process to identify what a leader must do for a team and to ask the group to consider what skills they thought that a leader must have in order to be successful. Naturally, they named traits such as 'good listener, fair, smart, cooperative, communicator, friendly, trustworthy'. To which I responded, "Now choose a leader that has as many of those qualities that you need for the success of the team." This process brought about high levels of anger and resentment as students were not considering others in their selection process.

Red-faced, furious Brian stomped his feet angrily over to me as his team deliberated as to who would become the team's leader for that particular activity. "This game isn't fair," he complained to me. "What's not fair about it?" I asked. "The leader choosing isn't fair, and I don't wanna play." "What exactly isn't fair about it," I continued to prod. "They aren't choosing me as the leader... I don't want to play" he shot back.

This incident reflects a sense of self-centered egoism in children but even more importantly, it also demonstrated that certain events and processes stir up emotions differently than others and differently between the participants. Brian eventually decided to play the game after I spoke to the team, apart from the rest of the class in the middle of the activity. His actions were clear to me that his emotions were taking control of his actions, which I pointed out to him may be the reason why the team hadn't considered him for the role of the leader for that particular activity.

Another instance that provokes emotion is the 'policing' of activities from one team to another. In the first week's activity, which involved a race to get from one end of the gym to another with a limited amount of resources, some students were more concerned with watching other teams to make sure that they follow the rules than they were concerned about their own success or failure.

In one particular case, one girl, Chelsea, who had risen to the role of the leader on her team, became so preoccupied with watching the other team for failure that it ultimately led to the failure of her own team. When she noticed the other team breaking the rules, a look came across her face like she was holding a winning lottery ticket. She was quick to report to me that the other team had broken the rules but her emotions became increasingly apparent as I told her that because I didn't see it, they didn't have to start over. Her frustration mounted and her entire team picked up on it and a noticeable apathy fell over the group when they believed that they didn't have a chance to win.

Win... and lose... are such strong emotional words for teams. Winning and losing are two simple words that carry a tremendous amount of meaning, especially emotional meaning to them. For instance, when we hear that someone won something, we are still well aware of how that person feels in association to the experience of winning. The same is true for losing; both winning and losing contain enormous emotional connotations. And this has certainly held true throughout the sessions this semester with both fourth and fifth graders.

The college students have noticed that the most obvious shifts and expressions of emotion occur at the end of the game or activity when a winner is declared and celebration ensues. When a deciding event occurs at the conclusion of a project, emotional swings occur. The desire to win invokes the most obvious emotion that is contagious between all of the members of a team and upon the other teams in the class. It is absolutely critical that a manager is empathic during emotional swings of success and failure on the work team.

Emotional Perception

Emotions are understood in a variety of ways; not to mention that they are misunderstood in even more ways. However, the key to empathy is being able to understand a person's emotion by reading and perceiving both verbal and non-verbal signals. Once we are able to understand our own emotions, as well as the ways in which we can regulate those emotions, then we can begin to understand how certain situations affect emotions in others. Empathy is a critical skill for the success of teams but it is a very difficult skill for many people to develop – especially children.

By week five of the 2+2=5 program, the children have their first exposure to the topic of emotional intelligence. The students had an activity in which they needed to get the entire team across a rope. Quickly, frustration with the activity turned to anger. The anger continued to mount until one student actually kicked another because of his failure in the activity. This shows that the students were not yet able to regulate their emotions properly. The important question that I posed to them was 'is anger a bad emotion?' Certainly, everyone was quick to agree that it was a bad emotion and could not have any positive effect on a team or in a team environment. I asked them to reconsider, thinking about the potential value of anger and other seemingly negative emotions. If anger is used properly, it can be channeled through regulation to act as a motivator both on a personal level and for the team as a whole.

Anger and frustration can contribute to the factors of motivation. The idea of self-motivation is critical to the overall scope of emotional intelligence. What or who motivates us? Quite often, anger can be the direct source by which we are motivated. Finding value in all types of motivation through self-regulation is one of the most critical components to emotional intelligence.

Following the discussion about the necessity of emotion regulation, the class was able to conclude that all emotions have different values; it is just how we use our emotions and regulate them that determine the effect that they have on us and our teammates. I remember one student commenting, "It's important to stop anger." After further discussion they were able to realize "anger isn't so bad if you use it right." A successful manager is able to harness anger and frustration on the team and use it to fuel progress on the work team.

Transference of Emotion

Most of the students began to realize quickly the ways in which our emotions are displayed with both body language and verbal cues, as well as how people understand others' emotion through empathy, but few students were conscious of their own emotions changing as the others around them would change. One of the most consistent occurrences in the observation of emotions is the ease of transference between the members of a team.

Emotions are contagious. There is no better example than the activity used to demonstrate the variety of different roles on teams. We played an activity called 'Line Soccer'. This is an activity in which two teams face each other along a line with a ball in the middle. Each student is given a number and each round begins with the facilitator calling off a number. The two students, one from each team, with that number, rush towards the ball in attempt to score a goal against the line of students that oppose them. The teams are instructed to evaluate the strengths and weaknesses of each member on the team and place them along the goal line strategically (slower, but bigger blockers towards the middle of the line and faster students along the ends of the line). The student leader of team one, Brian, then placed one particular boy, Steve, on the outside of the line of the team. Steve resisted Brian's demand and a quick argument broke out. Steve then went over to the side to which he was assigned and began to cry uncontrollably. I was the facilitator, and quite inconveniently, all alone and I had to think quickly.

Upon instruction, the team huddled for a meeting. I began by asking Steve why he thought Brian had put him in the position at the end of the line. He responded, through the tears, "Because he hates me. He never should have been the leader." Brian began to burst in, "Wait, no way…" I stopped Brian to ask him, "Why did you put him on the end?"

He stared blankly back at me stammering to find an answer. I then turned to Steve and said, "Today, Brian is the leader. The number one job of a leader is to make sure that his or her team is successful. I bet that he put you there because he thought that would give the team the best chance of winning." I asked him what skills he thought that he had in order to be put on the end. He couldn't come up with anything to which I told him that he was one of the fastest on the team and his team was relying on him for the points that he would get them at that position.

By this time, Steve had stopped crying. He was actually excited for the game. The entire dynamic on the team had changed in an instant. I noticed a negative energy on the team and through the team discussion, we were able to infuse a more positive emotion on the team, changing the whole emotional composure of not just the involved team members, but the whole team.

The game started. The team with the initial conflict scored the goal for the first four rounds. With each passing round, the confidence of the entire team rose with giant leaps and bounds. High fives, smiles, applause, and encouragement were all part of the team chemistry after the game had begun. Primarily, the emotion, once staunchly negative, quickly rippled through the team due to two events: the injection of positive emotion into the team in a negative situation and the accumulation of success during the activity. No greater and more acute change in emotion was more notably obvious than with Steve and Brian who now were congratulating each other, with high fives, after the team victory.

In stark contrast, team two experienced a similar transfer of emotion during the line soccer activity. As each round passed, team two became increasingly discouraged with each other as they lost round after round. One student, noticeably discouraged with the losing, began to pass blame on the other teammates. Those teammates began to reflect to discouraged emotion, one after another. Before long, the whole team was discouraged with each other, blaming each other for the negative results.

One of the most critical concepts for the team emotion is called the emotional economy.[3] Emotional economy is the sum emotion among the members of a team. As a result of the contagious emotion, the entire emotion of the team swayed one way or another depending upon the expression of emotion by outward members on the team. Due to the competitive nature of teams in an effort to beat each other in the activities, I noticed that the emotional economy of the teams had opposite effects upon each of the two teams. As one team was winning, emotions were high and excited. In

---

[3] "Emotional economy termed by Daniel Goleman in *Working with Emotional Intelligence*

contrast, the other team, who was losing, became discouraged and distraught.

It is critical for managers of teams to realize the ease in which emotion can be transferred between members of a team. If a team is unaware that emotions play a significant role in their success or failure, then they are susceptible to an emotional hijacking. Sometimes a hijacking can be so strong and influential that it completely derails the team from their current path.

There is no better example of an emotional hijacking than the Building Bridges activity referenced in the Negotiation chapter. The team of four fifth graders was assigned to come up with a strategy to build a bridge at least three feet long with only one newspaper and ten feet of scotch tape. Each of the four members on the team was required to accept one of the four positions available on the team: leader, communicator, problem solver, and resource manager. The job of the resource manager was to regulate the use of the limited tape and newspaper.

One team came up with an excellent strategy to build the bridge with cross-supports. Unfortunately, the team did not control the tape properly and the team ran out midway into the construction process. The team called me over for some additional tape. The facilitator told them that they couldn't have anymore. The team then ganged up against Erika, who had that job of controlling the use of the tape. Erika lashed back saying, "You're the ones that asked me for the tape." I left the team because I was more interested to see how the team would handle the situation as a team. Within a

EMOTIONAL INTELLIGENCE

short period of time one student kicked over the structure and no one was talking to Erika. So, again the facilitator went to intervene and held a meeting with the team, convincing the team to take stock of the situation and adjust their strategy accordingly.

The team discussed this possibility, after taking a minute to re-strategize. After reconsidering, the team went back to the drawing board and found a way to recover some of the supplies. The team discovered a new approach and instantly, they were once again excited at the possibility of rebuilding the bridge. After negotiation, the team once again had some tape, with which they were much more careful! The team began to work closer together, as a team, than they had ever during the activity. The entire emotion of the team had been completely changed. The team of fourth grade children working on the newspaper bridge activity provided a perfect example of how emotion can make or break the success of a team, if it isn't properly managed.

Leveraging Emotions

On the first day of the program, the business student facilitator was introducing the basics of teams and outlining some of the skills that we would be targeting during the seven weeks of the program. We then began the "End of the Line" activity in which the students had to get from one end of the gym to another without stepping on the floor, using a limited number of stepping stones. One of the leaders of a team, Rachel, started getting very frustrated and irritated when her teammates weren't listening to her idea for the strategy of the task.

Rachel was displaying a high level of emotion.

After seeing the negative emotion, the facilitators grew discouraged. I began thinking, 'I guess they don't understand much about teams if they are yelling at each other.' Naturally, I was frustrated with the negative emotion on the teams. After further consideration, I thought that the emotion, although negative, was important for the activity. Considering the commentary by Daniel Goleman, in *Emotional Intelligence,* he noted that students learn better in high emotion situations. This is an important point and most certainly an encouraging and uplifting one when challenging emotions arise on the team. Leaders should consider the different effects of high emotion situations and low-no emotion situations for teams. Most leaders much prefer some negative emotion, if they can harness it, as opposed to no emotion leading to a sense of apathy, certain to ripple through the team.

There is a wide variety of degrees of emotion for teams but perhaps apathy can be the most infectious killer of any team spirit. When even one team member doesn't care about the success or failure of the team, then that feeling quickly tends to spread through any team. Dangerous apathy erodes a team as a silent killer. It is a silent killer because it doesn't require a verbal conflict or physical altercation to interrupt the team. Only a lack of involvement from any team member can cause the ultimate failure of the team.

One student, Eric, had a generally negative attitude throughout nearly every week of the program. He generally interrupted each activity, saying something to

EMOTIONAL INTELLIGENCE

the effect of, "Can't we just play kickball? What's the point of this game, anyway?" It hardly affected the class until the teams were divided. Then, Eric's negative attitude always brought his team down. In every activity, his team usually finished last, if at all. He distracted his teammates with his lethargy and disrupted any interest his teammates may have had for the activity, regardless of the skill being developed or the activity.

Then one week, amid pressure from his teammates, Eric transformed and his team flourished. During the week in which we isolated team trust he came out of his apathetic shell. The activity was one in which all of the members of the class had to arrange themselves in a circle, each person facing the back of the person in front of them. Then, all at once, the class was required to sit down on the lap of the person behind them. Without a doubt, Eric did not trust his classmates. He specifically did not trust that the person behind him would be there to sit down on. So he hesitated. He didn't sit down as the rest of the class did; rather he leaned back in attempt to appease me that he made an effort. The person in front of him then fell to the ground, as there was no one to sit down on behind him, because of Eric's apathy and distrusting nature.

Then the change occurred. The person in front of him, Mark, after falling to the ground, got up and looked Eric straight in the eye and said, "I trusted you to be there, Eric. I fell because of you." The next attempt was successful and Eric had displayed a completely different attitude during the rest of the session, which involved trust falls. Perhaps the most satisfying experience during the entire program was the change that occurred in Eric and the sustained change that I observed throughout the final three weeks.

Upon reflection about the lack of emotion from Eric and how contagious it had been, I began to realize how easily emotions are displaced amongst the entire team quickly. There is rarely a strong, biting difference of emotion on a small team unless it is between two distinct leaders on the team.

In this case, the emotions of the team are being stirred up in such a way that the rest of the team must choose which leader to follow emotionally. This creates somewhat of a bottleneck effect in which the emotion brews, creating a rift in the team, resulting in alliances and other separations. In this way, teams must regulate their emotion in order to stimulate the team emotion enough in their group, yet manage the emotion properly in order to avoid rifts in the team caused by conflicting emotion. Children have demonstrated that managing emotion can be a delicate balance.

CHAPTER TWO

TEAM TRUST

"Trust is always number one. We just can't win if we don't trust each other." - **Bridget, fifth grade**

A Day in the Office

Warren leads a highly effective manufacturing team. Each team member knows their role and performs their role on the team at the highest level. Ryan, a team member, prepares the raw materials for the first stage of development. Rose, another team member, is responsible for stage two of the manufacturing process. Rose had a personal matter to address in the afternoon on Tuesday and would needs leave early. Upon her request, Ryan agreed to help Rose by completing her tasks while she was out for the afternoon. Ryan began to help Rose but quickly realized that he couldn't keep up with his own work. After an hour, Ryan gave up on Rose's work as he could barely keep up with his own responsibilities. Work began to pile up at Rose's station. Seven other team members on the production floor were now at a standstill because they relied on Rose's output to complete their own work. When she returned, the next morning, Rose realized that Ryan had not helped her as he agreed. Although these responsibilities were outside of

TEAM TRUST

Ryan's team role, it is critical that each team member maintain the big picture of the team goal in their mind and not just one's own individual role. Ryan didn't consider the impact that his actions would have on the level of team trust at the plant.

When Rose saw that Ryan had not kept his promise, she immediately felt a sense of distrust for him. She did not care about his reason for not keeping his word; she just knew that he had not kept it. The trust that the team had developed over the course of the project was shattered in an instant. Trust is something that is difficult to develop over long periods of time and easy to lose in an instant. When asked how to define trust, Nicole, a fourth grade student said "I used to think trust is like not telling a secret that your friend tells you, but it's much more than that. Trust is doing what you say you will do, when you say you will do it and being there for someone who is counting on you."

Managers must make a commitment to developing trust on their work teams. It is essential that managers put their employees in a position to develop team trust through exercises. Developing trust on a team is a lot like building muscle. You can't develop muscle unless you make a commitment to the gym every day. You can't develop trust unless you exercise that muscle each day. Building trust takes effort and can be developed within their team using simple activities. These activities alone will not fully develop the level of trust needed for high performing teams but it will begin the conversation about the importance of trust for the team and how trust can be built.

Knee Sit Activity

Team members stand in a circle, all team members must stand facing the back of the person to their right such that each person is looking at the back of the person in front of them, no person is face to face with another, all standing in a circle. The circle must be tight enough such that each person is no more than 8-10 inches apart from each other. Each person should be comfortably able to put their hands on the shoulders of the person in front of them.

Each person looks inward toward the center of the circle. At the direction of the facilitator, everyone in the team sits at once on the lap of the person behind him. The entire team is seated together mutually supported. This activity may take several attempts depending on the level of trust developed within the team.

Reflection Questions: Please note that the following questions can be used by the facilitator to help lead the reflection discussion after the activity is completed. Facilitators can use these questions or other questions generated as a result of the observations from the activity.

- Were you able to trust the person behind you to be there when you sat down?
- Did you consider the level of trust that the person in front of you had for you?
- Describe the trust that was built as the activity was being completed? How was trust developed in this

TEAM TRUST

activity and how do we develop trust in our team everyday?
- What barriers do people have to trusting others and how do we overcome those barriers?
- How important is trust to your work team?

Trust Fall Activity[4]

This activity should not be completed without thoroughly reading and understanding the safety precautions and discussing them with the co-facilitators so that each facilitator completely understands the activity and the procedure of completion. It is important to emphasize how serious the trust fall activity is to ten to eleven year-olds. It can also be important to emphasize this significant point to professionals. The facilitator can introduce the activity by reading:

"We have completed a lot of activities that have to do with teamwork, leadership, and communication. However, the trust fall is not a game. It is a very serious activity. Each person in the room is responsible to everyone in the room and must take this very seriously. You must pay full attention to the directions. Before we begin the activity, it is important to discuss a few important questions."

Pre-activity Reflection Questions: Please note that the following questions can be used by the facilitator to help lead the reflection discussion before the activity is completed. Facilitators can use these questions or other questions generated as a result of the observations from the activity.

---

[4] Please note, the 2+2=5 program and Scott Morency strongly encourages the use of the trust fall activity only with a trained professional. Scott Morency and/or the 2+2=5 program disclaim any liability for injury, death or damage to property.

- What is trust? Define what it means to you and its importance to our organization.
- Why is it important to have trust on a team?
- How can trust impact the performance of a team?
- How do we get others to trust us? How can trust be developed and how is trust lost?
- What are the potential consequences of losing trust on a team?

Activity setup:

Have the observers (not participating) stand approximately ten feet away from the falling platform. Ask for eight volunteers to start the activity. One person (the faller) is on the stage facing away from the catching team. Seven others are in the formation as follows:

Three students form a line shoulder to shoulder, facing another line of three students. One student stands at the end. The students put their arms out to "catch". Each arm should be aligned "every other" with the person across from them. No one person has their two arms next to each other. The person in the back is responsible for supporting the head of the trust faller. The two people closest to the platform should stand about six inches from the platform. The catchers should stand with their knees bent slightly when in the catching position.

Demonstrate the proper falling technique to the entire class: arms crossed over chest to form an X. (touch shoulders, elbows against stomach). The trust fallers must keep their legs straight and fall back into the arms of the seven students only after the signal from the lead facilitator, which is further outlined below. It is important to tell them not to bend their legs. Most people have a tendency to try to "sit" into the people, which must be avoided because it does not distribute the weight evenly. The trust fallers must stand with their heels at the edge of the platform. Only fall back once you have heard "fall away" after the countdown from the lead facilitator.

Facilitator note: (Step by step instructions once the trust fall formation has been set up)

- Ask the catchers "Catchers, are you ready?"
- Each catcher must respond yes confidently.
- Ask the faller "faller, are you ready?" Wait for a yes.
- Then shout, "3...2...1... and... fall away."
- The faller falls back safely into the arms of the catching team.
- Then the team rotates in an organized fashion.

The team should follow up after the activity with a reflection discussion on trust and why it is important for individuals on a team to trust each other and its importance to the success of the organization. It is also important to reconsider the pre-activity reflection questions and discuss any differences in responses before and after the activity.

Blind Shapes Activity

Each team member receives a blindfold and places it over their eyes. The facilitator prepares a length of 40-50 feet of rope tied together in a circle. Each team member takes hold of a section of the rope.

The team elects a leader who does not put a blindfold on. The leader is the only person allowed to speak. The facilitator calls out a shape. For example "triangle"; with more difficult shapes for more advanced teams. The leader of the team calls out instructions to each team member as to where to move in order to form the designated shape with the rope.

This activity can be done with five or more team members and can be done with multiple teams. Teams can compete to be the first to complete the shape. The team should follow up after the activity with a reflection discussion on trust and why it is important for individuals on a team to trust each other and its importance to the success of each organization.

Reflection Questions: Please note that the following questions can be used by the facilitator to help lead the reflection discussion after the activity is completed. Facilitators can use these questions or other questions generated as a result of the observations from the activity.

- How did trust play a role in success or failure in this activity?
- How can teams develop trust in the workplace?

WHAT A CEO CAN LEARN FROM A 4th GRADER

- How do you think a lack of trust would prohibit a team's effectiveness?
- What was difficult or frustrating in this activity? Relate it to a workplace scenario.

Children on Trust

What is trust? Most people think of trust as a 25 cent word that sounds great, but is never really put into practice. Trust is the act of believing in others. Trust is more than a feeling for a moment; it is a priceless component of character. It is a value that can be earned, but not bought. Trust can turn an impossible situation into a real success. Trust is an ingredient that wins championships, wins new clients, and that retains customers, and that builds enthusiastic work teams. Sheena, a fifth grader said, "Trust is knowing that someone will be there for you when you need them." Even more simply, Emelio, a fourth grader, said, "Trust is doing what you are supposed to do, doing what you say you will do, when you say you will do it." He continued, "Trust is something like if you were home alone and your mom doesn't want you to go outside, she has to trust you to not go outside."

At one point or another, we have all heard about the importance of trust between team members and that trust is a critical component of all high performance teams. Yawn. Sure, trust is important, we'd all agree, but what is it really worth to a team's performance?

When asked if they trust the members of their team, many people would say yes. When we say that we trust our teammates, most people haven't really scratched the surface of what trust can really do for a team. That is because our understanding of trust is limited to the low level of trust that we automatically grant to each other. We generally grant people a small amount of trust after meeting someone. For the most part, we are able to trust people until they betray the trust. That is not to say that we trust everyone we meet on the street, but once we have met someone and develop a transactional relationship with someone, we have a basic level of trust.

My father always told me "For the most part, we all grant each other a certain level of trust. From that basic level of trust, we continue to build trust over time by doing what we say we will do and by extending trust to other members of the team. But once you've lost it, trust is so difficult to get back again."

When we say that we trust someone on our work team, we generally are referring to the moderate level of automatic trust that we grant to people that we interact with on a transactional basis. Real, deep underlying trust is built painstakingly slow over time and can be lost in the blink of an eye.

We often take for granted that certain minimal level of trust we have for others. On a work team, we trust our teammates to a certain level. Think about the coworkers on your team; how many of them do you really, truly trust to be there for the team at all times? What happens to that trust when one of your team members let the team down? When we think of trust, we rarely think about the genuine, deep trust that develops only after working at it over a sustained period of time. True well-developed trust revolves around completely trusting the character of others.

Fourth Graders on Trust

The fourth graders stood together in a circle; each student seeming anxious to perform the Knee Sit activity where each student was required to sit in a circle on the lap of the person behind them. There were plenty of looks of concern and distrust around the circle. After explaining to the students that they would be sitting on the lap of the person behind them, the children shot glances of fear around the room.

"I'm not gonna do that!"

"There's no way that we can do that!"

"I'm gonna get hurt because Billy just goofs off. He won't be there when I sit down."

"I don't trust *her*. Put me in front of Susie."

There was an obvious lack of trust around the room and the children had no problem expressing that sense of doubt and lack of trust. So before we began the activity, a discussion about trust and the importance of trust was critical. In this particular case, trust was built as we discussed the topic of responsibility to the team. The children taught the college students that even a simple conversation about trust helps to develop team trust. Rachel stood in front of Mary and Mary in front of Susie. If Mary did not fully trust Susie, she would not sit down on the lap of Susie. Mary had a responsibility to the team; to trust Susie or else Rachel and the rest of the team would fall. There are no partial successes in the "Knee Sit" activity, its all or nothing. Every single member of the circle must

TEAM TRUST

have complete trust in the team in order to be successful. In order for the activity to be successful everyone must trust the person behind them; any break in the trust would cause the entire team to fail.

Several failed attempts ensued as children sat down, spilling all over the floor and screaming. After a few failed attempts at the Knee Sit, the class needed to regroup and talk about all of the activities leading up to this particular "trust" week. The children taught the college facilitators that team skills are often interrelated and tend to build other skills. For example, being an effective communicator on the team allows others to develop trust in that person. A teammate who has gained the role of the leader has not done so unless the team members have an elevated level of trust in that person. Several children were able to share memories in which trust was built in other activities:

-"I remember when we did the Lava Walk and Bobby talked us through getting across the gym... we had to trust him and his idea or we would have never been able to get across the gym."

-"What about when Sarah was the leader last week, we had to trust her to be a good leader and to put the team first."

-"When Martin went to the other team to negotiate supplies, we had to trust that he was a good negotiator and that he would be able to get what we needed."

After discussing several ways in which the teams had developed trust throughout the last several weeks, the team was ready to try the Knee Sit activity again. On

WHAT A CEO CAN LEARN FROM A 4th GRADER

the very next attempt, the entire class sat together, each on the lap of the person behind them and immediately burst into excited hysteria. Building on the success, we tried the activity again and again and again, each time an immediate and complete success. Trust began rippling through the team; at first within a small section of the circle and ultimately the entire class would trust each other. The trust built an energy that I had not seen from that team throughout the entire program. Reflecting upon past team successes helps to build team trust.

When describing the Knee Sit activity to the class, no one thought it could be done. Little by little, people on the team began trusting each other and ultimately creating a dynamic that is rarely seen or experienced. In the beginning of the activity, maybe a few people on the team trusted and it was evident as certain portions of the circle would stay up for an extended moment or two. By the end of the activity, everyone on the team trusted each other without reserve. That high level of trust can only be built and earned, in time, as teams work more closely together. When someone explains that trust is important for teams, which is the high performance level of trust they are speaking of. Not just trust in the sense that one normally thinks of trust; true deep running trust throughout the entire team drives success.

The Trust Fall

Many of us have heard of, seen, or participated in a trust fall at some point. Now imagine being nine or ten year-olds and being told that you are about to fall backwards from five feet high into the arms of your classmates. That takes the highest level of trust, especially for a team of children. Anyone who thinks this might be easy hasn't spent a lot of time around screaming, excitable ten year-olds.

During one particular week, we ran the trust fall activity after becoming confident that trust had been developed over the last several week's activities. With the excitement of ten and eleven year-olds, the facilitator placed extra emphasis on the serious nature of the trust fall. The facilitator introduced the trust fall activity by saying, "Over the last nine weeks we have been doing many different activities. During those activities, the teams that trusted each other were the most successful. But in the trust fall activity, trust is more than just a nice side benefit. Trust is essential for success. Nothing about trust is easy, but you will be rewarded with something that you will remember for many, many years."

Students reluctantly line up for the trust fall. "Are there any volunteers to be first?" The facilitator might as well have asked if anyone wanted extra math homework for the night. One ambitious student finally stepped forward. The student climbed the stairs up to the stage approaching their fate on the trust fall.

"Do you trust your teammates to catch you?" The facilitator asks.

"Ugh, no not really."

"If you are going to do this, it's critical that you trust your teammates."

"Ok. I do trust them, but I'm still nervous."

After the first student completed the trust fall, the class exploded with excitement. Instantly, five more students were ready to volunteer to be next. After the second volunteer, all 26 students in the class were ready to volunteer to be next. It was evident that trust built more and more after each volunteer. The fourth grade class taught the facilitators that trust is built over time. Trust is not something that happens all at once and no matter how much we talk about trust, it is built more effectively through actions than words. And finally, the class taught the facilitators that trust is built through success. It is important for managers to harness both big and small successes as a tool for building trust.

Most managers would agree that it is important to develop trust on work teams, but how? Trust is often an elusive intangible. How does a high performance work team develop a rich sense of trust that is essential for success? Fourth and fifth grade students came up with some critical trust development points.

Understanding Your Role on the Team

It is critical that each member clearly understands what the team expects of them. If you understand your responsibilities to the team, the rest of the team will trust that you will fulfill your role. Demonstrate your understanding of your role in your interactions and communication with the team. You can build trust by simply showing that you understand the team's expectations of you. Trevor, a fourth grader said "It's important for each one of us to do what we are good at, to each have our own role and to stick to it. I am good at strategy and my team trusts me to do it because they have seen me do it each week." We must not only understand our own role but also be willing to help in any role on the team as it becomes necessary for team success.

Respect the Team

Respect is a key ingredient for trust development. Team members must always have a sense of respect for each of the other team members. This often becomes increasingly difficult, if not prohibitively difficult, in moments of frustration. Make sure that any criticism is directed constructively towards individuals on the team. Teammates must be charismatic in your communication and remember that respect drives team success. Team members will build trust in you if they feel that you respect them. Respect them and they will respect you; respect breads respect. A sense of mutual respect on a team will drive trust. Amanda added, "You can develop trust by believing in the person. The person acts and sticks up for you. We need to be nice and treat each other good. We trust each other."

Be Emotionally Intelligent

Trust is developed between people who understand each other and by responding to other's emotions and personalities. Team members must demonstrate empathy, understanding the emotions and work styles of individuals on the team. Emotional intelligence is inherently coupled with deepened levels of trust. Individual teammates must be responsive to other teammates' work needs.

In the trust fall activity, in which students would take turns falling backwards into the arms of their teammates from a height of about thirty-six inches. During the activity, the facilitator asked the catchers, "How do you think 'Billy' (the faller) feels right now?" The class began by responding with some noticeable uncertainty. No one seemed to know how he felt. The college student facilitator then asked them how they thought that could figure out exactly how Billy felt; including understanding what clues might be observable. One student then explicitly asked him how he felt; covering perhaps the most obvious way in which we can find out someone's emotions: asking them directly.

The facilitator then asked them further, "How can you tell what he is feeling without him telling you directly." In other words, what nonverbal behavioral characteristics can we observe to be empathic? How can we understand another team member's emotions? With time allowed for the children to analyze and discuss, the elementary students then concluded that Billy was nervous because of the shaky tone in his voice and the tense posture that he was showing as he stood, ready to fall into the trust fall.

With practice, the students quickly became more and more able to understand the emotions of their classmates. Soon they were able to observe and describe a range of emotions like "anxious, excited, nervous, and even uninterested." When it becomes obvious that other team members are making an effort to understand an individual's emotions, trust is developed within the team.

Communicate Effectively

The way in which we communicate presents an opportunity to build trust on a team. It is essential that team members are genuine in the way in which they communicate with their teammates. This means not only the way in which we speak but how we listen. Team members build trust by listening attentively and actively. When asked what communication is, Robbie, a fourth grader said, "Communication is more than just talking and talking… we tried that, everyone talked, no one listened, we got nowhere. We need to listen more than we talk. We need to listen and listen carefully." Robbie was exactly right; listening is critical to communication and building trust.

Follow Through

The importance of following through cannot be understated. Quite simply, following through means always doing what you say that you will do. Team members can develop trust by following through because individuals on the team will begin to form a sense of reliance and trust amongst teammates which will contribute in the long run. If you are constantly failing to do what you say you will do, team members will lose trust in you. We can build trust in ways as simply as arriving at meetings on time and prepared. Martin, a fourth grader, says, "Sean never pays attention to the directions, why should I trust him? How can I trust him?" If we always try to exceed the expectations of our team members and satisfy our responsibilities, then trust will naturally follow.

The way in which trust can impact a team's performance is limitless. When we fully trust our teammates to come through for the team, we are able to devote full focus to our team responsibilities. Without a strong sense of trust coupled with the other interpersonal values of the 2+2=5 program, a team can not reach its optimal performance. Trust builds a sense of team chemistry that triggers enthusiasm and energy. Jimmy, age nine, added, "If we're cooking a cake, trust is the icing that can get you that little extra. But if the frosting is no good, that's all anyone talks about."

CHAPTER THREE

CLEAR AND EFFECTIVE COMMUNICATION

"We communicate much more without our mouth than with it." - Jeff, fifth grade

A Day in the Office

Wendy is the senior manager at Apco, a professional services firm. She's been with the firm for 27 years and has seen a lot of interesting things in that time. She has built a fine career around being considered one of the most technically competent people in her field. Lately, however, she's been struggling with the new software that has come out that is "supposed" to make her job easier. She wishes things could just go back to the old way of doing things. She asks a new member of her team, Ryan, the fresh college recruit, to assist her with the software.

Within minutes the communication gap, between Ryan and Wendy, becomes palpable. Ryan shoots Wendy an instant message explaining to her how to operate the new software. He's using words Wendy has never even heard before. She's having trouble visualizing what he is talking about in the instant message. She wishes he had just come over to show her personally.

Effective communication in the workplace is the

CLEAR AND EFFECTIVE COMMUNICATION

primary building block to team success. Barriers to effective communication are often culturally driven, age gap driven, technology gap driven, and gender driven. Our understanding of these barriers can make us much better communicators, both as senders and receivers of communication. Managers can effectively develop communication skills in their teams by constantly providing opportunities for team members to develop their communication skills.

The opportunity to interact and communicate through a variety of different channels can be extremely effective. In addition, leading activities that handicap one channel of communication can help refine other channels. For example, in the 2+2=5 program, we often prohibit the team members from communicating verbally in order to sharpen and to become keenly aware of nonverbal communication skills. The facilitator may allow only the leader to talk in a certain activity, in order to hone the team members' critical listening abilities. The closing of one or more communication channels can often develop and refine other channels. Managers can use the following activities to develop communication skills on their teams:

Lava Walk Activity

Teams of four to five members stand at one end of a room. Each team receives one square foot of cardboard per person. The facilitator provides the following directions to the teams:

A volcano erupted here several hours ago and lava has covered the entire ground. We have hired you as a team of volcanic experts to rescue some expensive testing equipment on the other side of this room. As a team, you must get to the other side of the room and return with the testing equipment. All members of the team must cross together. Only the cardboard stepping pads will protect you from the lava. The pads may not be slid across the floor. If any one team member falls off any pad, the entire team must restart at the beginning.

Reflection Questions: Please note that the following questions can be used by the facilitator to help lead the reflection discussion after the activity is completed. Facilitators can use these questions or other questions generated as a result of the observations from the activity.

- Describe the team communication when developing a strategy for this activity.
- In what ways could the team have communicated more effectively?
- What nonverbal communication techniques were used during this activity?
- What role does nonverbal communication play in our

CLEAR AND EFFECTIVE COMMUNICATION

everyday lives?
- How should communication techniques used by managers be adapted to reflect the unique dynamic of each team?

Hear it, Tell it Activity

This activity is a variation of the children's game "telephone." However, this activity provides the opportunity to observe the changes from generation to generation. Ask for 5 volunteers. The first volunteer remains in the room while the other four exit the room. The facilitator reads an excerpt to the first volunteer and the remaining observers. The 2+2=5 program uses the following excerpt; however any detailed excerpt would suffice.

Derek Johnson was having a terrible day, only twelve days before his eighth birthday. He was in the second grade at the John F. Kennedy Elementary School. His class had a spelling bee and he lost on the last word, "banana". He spelt it with one too many n's. Then he got his geography quiz back; he only got a C when he was hoping to get at least a B. On his way home, he got in a fight with his best friend, Curtis, who he had an argument with over Pokemon. Then, after the fight, he ran into Billy the Bully who stole his Sponge Bob lunch box. Finally, when he got home, his day had improved. He opened the door to find his new puppy waiting at the door for him. He instantly ran outside to the backyard to play catch with his new puppy, Spots.

The first volunteer must retell the story, with as much detail as possible to the second volunteer. The second volunteer enters the room and hears the story for the first time. Then the second volunteer retells the story to the third volunteer with as much detail as possible. The observers carefully note changes and omissions in the story.

Reflection Questions: Please note that the following questions can be used by the facilitator to help lead the reflection discussion after the activity is completed. Facilitators can use these questions or other questions generated as a result of the observations from the activity.

- Which details were easiest to remember? Were the details at the beginning or the end easier to remember; in the middle?
- When thinking about what details were easiest to remember, what does that tell us about how to be effective communicators?
- What does that tell us about effective communication?
- How did emotion play a role in the changes of the story?
- What specific listening techniques did you observe that were helpful?
- How will our observations impact the way we communicate verbally, in writing, on the phone, in person, and/or non-verbally?

CLEAR AND EFFECTIVE COMMUNICATION

Blind Line Activity

This activity is quick and simple, but provides an excellent opportunity to exercise communication skills that we normally do not consider. The facilitator should bring one blindfold for each team participant.

If there are ten people on the team, place the numbers 1-10 on slips of paper in a bag or hat. There should be one number for each member of the team. Have each person select a number from the bag and look at it without showing anyone else. Then each team member must put a blindfold on. The team is then instructed to get in a line in numerical order without speaking or seeing their teammates. At the facilitator's choosing, the team may have two minutes to discuss a strategy without sharing their numbers with the rest of the team.

This activity works best with two teams to allow for a race between the two teams to get in numerical order. The facilitator should observe techniques used and reactions to the activity to discuss in the post-activity reflection.

Reflection Questions: Please note that the following questions can be used by the facilitator to help lead the reflection discussion after the activity is completed. Facilitators can use these questions or other questions generated as a result of the observations from the activity.

- Describe how it felt to have your senses limited in this

activity.
- How do we unknowingly "handicap" our communication in the everyday workplace?
- How did the teams communicate without speaking? How did you come up with the strategy?
- What would have made this activity easier?
- What can we do in the workplace to make our communication more clear and effective?

Clear and Effective Communication

Paramount to a team's success is the ability to communicate well with each other. One of the most important ways that groups are able to turn into high performance teams is through seamless communication. When asking fourth graders to define communication, Hannah, age thirteen, explained, "Communication is listening." After being startled by that answer, the facilitator probed further,

"Great, a big part of communication is about being a good listener. Could you explain more about what you mean by that?" I asked.

"Well, it's easy to talk, everyone talks and it got us nowhere. No one listened. People forget, it is sometimes more important to listen," she replied.

Clear and effective communication strikes a sense of balance between listening and speaking while being keenly conscious of the elements of nonverbal communication. The fourth and fifth grade students were able to discover and discuss important tips for being better listeners, more adept speakers, and being more attentive to nonverbal communication such as body language.

Being an Active Listener

Many people find it challenging to listen attentively because of the way our brain processes communication. People can speak an average of 130 words per minute; however, listeners have the ability to hear and process between four and five times the number of words per minute.[5]

---

[5] Boyd, S.D. (2001). The human side of teaching: Effective listening. *Techniques: Connecting Education & Careers, 76* (7), 60-61.

When we listen to a speaker, at an average rate of 130 words per minute, our brain has additional unused capacity: a void. In order to use that additional capacity, listeners find themselves thinking about other things such as thinking about how they will respond to the speaker after they have finished. Listeners also think of many other things such as planning for a meeting later in the afternoon or even what they will have for lunch.

Although it seems nearly impossible to identify these situations when reflecting on previous conversations, the next time you are involved in a conversation with someone, pay attention to how many times you drift in a conversation or begin thinking about your response before the other person has finished speaking. This can be called response rehearsing. Response rehearsing is one of the biggest barriers to listening. Many people also try to anticipate what the person will say next; causing them to miss what is actually being said. Hannah, age twelve, further developed our understanding of the importance of being a good listener by saying, "We clarified the goal by listening so that we were all on the same page and knew what to do." Brian, her teammate added, "We needed each person to understand the strategy or else this couldn't be done. If even one person didn't listen, the team would have failed."

While there are certainly environmental barriers to good listening, there are several ways to improve one's listening skills. When you picture a typical fourth grade classroom, we typically don't associate that image with a room full of good listeners. Ask any fourth grade teacher if his or her students are strong listeners and I bet

CLEAR AND EFFECTIVE COMMUNICATION

the majority of teachers would say no.

Surprisingly, in the unique 2+2=5 environment, children had some incredible ideas on how to become better listeners and more effective communicators overall. It is important that all members of the team are good listeners and strong communicators and may utilize the following methods, devised by ten and eleven year-olds to improve communication skills:

Making Eye Contact

Making sustained eye contact with the speaker is the most effective way to ensure the speaker that you are listening attentively. Eye contact signals that you are genuinely interested in what the speaker has to say. In addition, eye contact is a good way to maintain focus and avoid distractions. "I can tell he's not listening to me, he's not even looking at me," Juliet, a fourth grader observed. When we are speaking to someone and they are not making eye contact, it is easy to assume that they are disinterested. It's important to be conscious of the level of eye contact that we make with a speaker because of the messages that we are sending with our eye contact.

Maintain Open Body Posture

Open body posture quite simply consists of physically facing your body toward the speaker. This seems like a pretty simple thing, but it can be so vital for effective communication as it shows the speaker that they have your attention. Imagine walking into a room to tell a coworker about a very important deadline. You call his name and begin to advise him of the deadline. His desk is situated facing the window and he continues to stare down at his computer screen with his back towards you. You call his name again. He finally turns his neck and looks at you but remains closed leaving his body to face to desk. As a speaker, he is sending you a signal that he might not be fully listening to what you are saying or is simply disinterested. We can show others that we are truly listening to them if we completely turn our bodies to face them as they are speaking. Maintaining open body posture is not something we normally think of, but it can be very effective for strong communication skills.

Paraphrasing

An effective way to ensure speakers that you are listening is to paraphrase what they are saying. This is something that most of us find easy to understand, but few actually use this skill when communicating. For example:

"Rita, could you please be sure to complete the TPS file. I really need to get that file over to the New York office as soon as possible. I'm starting to feel like this client is more work than they are worth. Perhaps we should have charged a higher fee. Well anyway, it's nearing lunch time."

"So what you're saying is, you'd like me to make the TPS file my top priority?"

"Thank you Rita. That's exactly what I'm saying."

Speakers will be appreciative that you are acknowledging that you are genuinely listening, but also will be more confident that you understand what they have said to you. It is important to remember to paraphrase rather than just mechanically repeat what was said, often referred to as parroting, which carries a risk of being offensive.

The most important communication lesson that the college business student facilitators learned from the fourth graders is the importance of being a good listener and its direct relationship to the success of a team. During the "Lava Walk" activity, as several teams had repeated the activity, difficulty and frustration continued to mount, failure after failure. Each member of the team, growing more frustrated, started to yell at each other and speak over each other to the point that no one on the team was really listening to each other as the problems and tensions mounted.

Finally, one of the children suggested that each team select one designated leader who could speak but everyone else was forced to remain silent and listen to the leader. This change brought about instant success. Suddenly, everyone on the team was forced to listen to the leader. After completing the activity under this modification, facilitators tried the activity again, allowing everyone to talk. However, this time, children remained quiet, speaking and listening more carefully. The children were more able to follow directions of the leader, allowing the team to be on the same page strategically.

Effective Speaking

One activity in which children were able to teach the facilitators about effective speaking was the "Hear it, Tell it" activity. The children are responsible for relaying a detailed short story from person to person. All of the other students, not participating, take observation notes, paying careful attention to how each person speaks. During a reflection, the children shared what they thought were some of the best ways of speaking in order to get your message across. Nathan made this observation, "It's obvious why Mary was able to remember the most about the story. It's because Sheila was telling the story well. I noticed that she made faces, she used her hands, she stood closer to make points. Sheila was the best speaker." One fifth grader, Manny, added, "Until now, I didn't think it mattered so much the way we speak. I just thought words are words." The truth is that the way in which we speak is often worth more and has a bigger impact than the actual words that come out of our mouths.

There are several techniques used by effective speakers when speaking in small teams or in one on one situations. The way in which the ten and eleven year-olds interacted showed that there were several techniques that can be employed to be a more effective speaker. People who master these speaking techniques are more likely to find team and individual success. These skills include speaking with passion, using body language effectively, and being clear and concise in the way that you speak.

Speak with Passion

If you reflect energy when you speak, you are more likely to capture the attention of your audience. Effective speakers use changes in pitch and tone in order to reflect emotion and passion in spoken words. "I think Bobby should be the leader, he's always enthusiastic," said Jeff, age twelve. Effective speakers use energy to build support for what they are saying. Think about the people that you know that you really enjoy listening to, either at work or in social situations. Think about the level of enthusiasm and passion that which they speak and try to build that passion into your speaking technique. Passion breeds success, and will quickly spread throughout your team. Professional speakers call this technique "inflection" which typically involves a change in pitch, tone, or speed in order to attract the interest of the listeners.

Use Body Language Effectively

Another aspect of effective speaking includes using body language to accentuate and emphasize certain points. Effective speakers use hand gestures, facial expressions, and body positioning to increase the effectiveness of the speaker. That is not to say that effective speakers flail their arms as they speak; there is a limit to the amount of body language we use. When used improperly, body language can be distracting and detract from what the speaker is saying. It is important that we are careful not to use too many gestures that distract the listener from the message.

Be Clear and Concise

Think about the last time you listened to someone drag on and on with insignificant details and unnecessary tangents. You probably found yourself saying, "Alright, already, cut to the chase." Think about that moment the next time you're the speaker. It detracts from the message when the speaker provides unnecessary details or side commentary that seems to drone on and on.

Effective speakers keep their message clear and concise, providing only necessary details to the message and enough detail that is relevant and necessary. The audience is more likely to understand the key points to what you are saying if the speaker keeps it clear and concise. During the fourth grade activity, frustrated Sydney said to his teammate, "Why do you talk so much? Just tell me what I need to know." Sydney, found a nice way to say "shut up," but little did he know that he was onto something. I think many professionals would agree with Sydney, age twelve, that it is better to get right to the point. Many managers agree that if anything is worth saying at all, it can be summed up in one page or less. We should speak in the same way, focus on the important points. Effective speakers focus on trimming the fat and keeping just the facts and the necessary details. Pithy conversation is effective and efficient.

Communication is to a high performing team as oil is the lifeblood of a car. It keeps a team running smoothly and is critical for all components of the team. Effective communication is essential to a team's success and one of the primary building blocks of high performance teams. Freddie, age thirteen, summed it up best by saying, "Communication is not just important for teams; it is important in all other parts of life: at home, with my brother, at recess. We are always communicating, whether we know it or not." Indeed, Freddie was exactly

CLEAR AND EFFECTIVE COMMUNICATION

right. Every second of every day, we are communicating something verbally in the actual words, in our tones, in our silences, in our facial expressions, in our gestures, in our dress and appearance, and in our posture. As we become more and more conscious of the verbal and nonverbal messages that we are sending and more acutely aware of the messages that are sent to us, we will become much more effective communicators. This is a critical attribute of any high performing team.

Be Conscious of Technology Barriers

Many people in their 20's or even 30's don't hesitate to use email, text messaging, and instant messaging as a primary means of communication. Those that have grown up with this technology use it as the main vehicle for communication. The use of technology is often the quickest, most convenient and efficient way of communicating. However, it's important to consider the fact that the effectiveness of technology driven communication is called into question in two major ways.

First, there is a definite technology barrier based on the level of familiarity between different generations. Those in their 20's and even 30's grew up with a lot of this technology at their fingertips. Many people 40 and over are willing and able to use these channels of communication, but there are also many others that are quite averse to using these technologies as a primary means of communication. It is important to remember that there may be generational gaps in your work environment where more senior members of the company prefer face to face conversation or at least a telephone conversation.

Secondly, when we use email, text messaging, and instant messaging, we are favoring a quick, convenient, instant communication, but we must consider that we are sacrificing some primary elements of communication. Effective communicators understand that the actual words that are spoken only amount to about 10% of what we are communicating. The other 90% of our communication comes from our tone, voice inflection and emphasis, body language, gestures, and posture; these are all components of communication that are completely lost in an email or instant message. Ultimately, technology can be a facilitator of communication or a barrier to communication. We must be fully conscious about how we leverage technology as a communication resource and understand how that vehicle of communication is being received by the other person.

Think back to the last time you received an email where there may have been a misunderstanding that could have been avoided with a phone call or face to face visit. We must be conscious that emails, text messages, and instant messages come with an inherent price: misunderstandings. If we are aware of these potential pitfalls, we can be more effective in our electronic communication and understand the appropriateness and necessity of face to face conversation for certain situations.

Communication truly is the oil in a car. It keeps a team running smoothly. It's not something that we think of as being a critical component of teambuilding but it's

CLEAR AND EFFECTIVE COMMUNICATION

the foundation that we hardly ever think about. Most of us think about the oil in our cars about once every three months. If communication is so critical to effective team-building, we must be more conscious about the ways in which we communicate. We must think about communication as not only speaking but also communicating non-verbally and actively listening. We send signals each moment of every day. Team members have an acute ability to pick up on these signals so we must be sure that what we communicate is truly what we intend. Marilyn, age fifteen concluded, "Communication seems so simple, but there's a lot more to it. There's a lot to think about."

CHAPTER FOUR

LEADERSHIP

"A leader steers the ship" - Megan, fourth grade

Sure, we all know that in order for any team to be successful, it must have a leader who goes beyond the role of a manager to actually lead the team from the trenches. It's not exactly astute to say that a manager manages and a leader leads but it is important to recognize that these are two different skills. Teams need leaders. Teams rely on their leaders. Everyone knows that leadership is important but how can leadership be at its utmost effectiveness? Many people say that leaders are born not made. In many ways, this is true as some of the necessary skills to be an effective leader are naturally bred within leaders. However, these raw skills must be refined through dedicated development.

Observing children take part in 2+2=5 leadership activities revealed an important point to be made about effective leadership. The children demonstrated the importance of leading by example. How many times have you been barked an order from a manager and thought to yourself, "They're just getting rid of something they wouldn't do themselves." If a manager is down in the trenches with the team, the members of the team will have exponentially more respect for the team leadership and be more inclined to follow the leadership without reserve. Teams absolutely need leaders that are willing to walk in the shoes of their team members. Leading by example is one of the simplest ways in which a leader can gain the following of their team members.

Another lesson that the fourth graders demonstrated was that leaders must be flexible in their role on the team. "As the leader of the team, Lisa had to adjust to where the team needed her," Kim, age eleven, said. Kim noticed during one of the activities that everyone wanted to perform one particular task leaving other tasks unattended. As a leader, she had to adjust her role in order to balance the team.

A Day in the Office

Mary is the manager of a fast paced, high volume bar and restaurant. It's a Friday night and the restaurant is extremely busy. Mary is an excellent manager. She constantly has her finger on the pulse of her staff. Within minutes, Mary recognizes a service backup in the kitchen. One of the staff members, a dishwasher, did not show up for their shift. Mary called the on-call dishwasher and he couldn't come in right away. Mary knew that if they didn't have a dishwasher immediately, the kitchen couldn't function and plates would continue to pile up. Eventually they wouldn't be able to get any more orders out.

Mary could have said, "That's not my job, I'm the manager. I'll get Rex to wash dishes." Mary recognized the need in the line and jumped up to the dishwasher to clear the backlog. A successful manager and team leader needs to see the big picture from all angles. Specifically, a leader needs to understand the role of each team member. A leader's role is not to sit in a tower and point out the things that are wrong. A leader must be willing and able to take on any role in the team as it becomes necessary to the team's success. Sometimes a leader's most critical role is to be humble enough to step back and be a follower on the team. The leader occasionally becomes a follower in order to develop the skills of the team members who are able to demonstrate that level of leadership in certain situations.

Indeed fourth and fifth graders taught the business student facilitators two important lessons on leadership: lead by example and leaders must be flexible, even if it means stepping back and being a follower. As the children were first learning the importance of leadership, nearly every single child wanted to be chosen as the leader. Everyone wanted to be the leader because of their view that it carried with it the glorious title of "leader". As the activities progressed, the children realized that true leaders don't need the title and are willing to step away from the forefront, the limelight, if it becomes necessary for the team's success.

These lessons are far better experienced than read. Team members can really only learn effective leadership techniques by having the opportunity to exercise these skills. There's no better way to learn leadership skills than to be put in a leadership role in a pressurized situation. Team members, who are not necessarily the designated team leader, can and should have the opportunity to serve in a leadership capacity

LEADERSHIP

when their skill set coincides with the team's challenge, called situational leadership. Managers can better prepare their team members for leadership opportunities on their teams by using 2+2=5 activities such as the following:

Run of the Blob Activity

This game is a variation of the popular children's game "tag". One person starts off as the "it", also known as the blob. The blob is central to the activity and ultimately the designated leader. The "blob" then begins to chase members around the playing field, while trying to tag them. Once they have tagged another player, that player must join the "blob," required to hold hands with the end of the "blob."

The blob will continue to try and make tags of the remaining players while the blob becomes bigger and bigger as the activity continues. The blob must not break hands, even to make a tag; only tags made with the hands of the players on the end of the blob are legal tags. Players tagged by the blob must join at the end in which they were tagged. The activity is complete once everyone has been tagged by the blob. If the blob breaks apart at any time, it must begin again with an individual blob.

Reflection Questions: Please note that the following questions can be used by the facilitator to help lead the reflection discussion after the activity is completed. Facilitators can use these questions or other questions generated as a result of the observations from the activity.

- Did the activity become easier or more difficult as the blob grew in size? Why?
- Was there a leadership presence on the blob? How did

he or she become the leader?
- What does this activity tell us about effective leadership and how does it challenge us to think about our own leadership techniques?
- How does environment, task, personality and team dynamic impact the type of leadership that is effective in a given situation?

Human Knot Activity

Teams of at least eight members stand in a circle facing inward. Each team member stretches their arms inward and holds the hand of two different people across the circle. Each person must be holding two different hands other than someone directly next to them. This entanglement has tied the human knot. Team members must work together climbing through, under, and over arms in order to untangle the human knot. Variations on this activity include completing the activity without talking or with only the designated leader allowed to speak.

Reflection Questions: Please note that the following questions can be used by the facilitator to help lead the reflection discussion after the activity is completed. Facilitators can use these questions or other questions generated as a result of the observations from the activity.

- What are some important qualities that teams look for in a leader?
- What role did leadership play in this activity?
- What does this activity tell us about effective leadership techniques?
- Were there multiple people on the team that served in a leadership capacity?
- How do multiple leaders impact an activity?
- Is it important to have a designated, official leader before beginning an activity?

Effective Leadership

The Run of the Blob is often the most frustrating activity for the college student facilitators. Team members must join the blob once they are tagged. Individual team members join the blob by joining hands with the person at one of the ends of the blob. The team members must continue to hold hands as they move as a team to capture the remaining team members who attempt to evade the blob. Often times, the team of children get so excitable that the Blob starts moving in opposite directions and ultimately the blob splits apart in one section as each end of the blob heads in an opposite direction.

Shawn was the blob leader. As the game went on and on, the blob would get bigger and bigger with each person that was tagged. Ultimately, the blob would break apart in excitement causing the team to have to start over again. Shawn became more and more frustrated with the team each time they were forced to start over. After about three or four unsuccessful attempts, we talked as a class about how leadership could be important in this activity. As the blob leader, Shawn did not have any ideas about how he could demonstrate leadership in the blob. As a team, we talked further about how a leader gives direction to the team. Kathryn, age ten, said, "A leader is a person that has good ideas and listens to our team's suggestions. It's important to have a leader so your team stays in order." Shawn began to listen to the suggestions of his classmates. Vinisha said, "Since you're the leader, why don't you call off where you want us to go, say left, right, faster, slower." Shawn liked this idea and the activity began again. Shawn began calling out left, right and so on.

Then something amazing happened. I noticed that the blob was getting bigger and bigger, about fifteen or so children and they were having a hard time hearing Shawn's direction. Remarkably, Shawn remembered a lesson from a previous week about strategy. As a result, Shawn called the blob in for a huddle at which point the team made a strategy. This sounds pretty logical to professionals, but a group of screaming fourth graders forming a strategy, unprovoked by the college facilitator, was truly amazing.

Because the facilitators had used experiential learning through the team builders, the lesson was ingrained in the children and they followed the lesson without direction from the facilitators. This was a testament to the power of experiential learning. Business managers can talk for hours to their employees about the importance of strategic development, but if it is emphasized through activities and demonstrated in practice, these "single acts" ultimately become "behaviors" that are a part of the team character. "A leader is someone who not only leads the team but is a person who listens and respects the ideas of the team members," added Vinisha again.

2+2=5's Shining Moment

Sometimes, when we expect one result, we get something completely different; and in the end, we are far more amazed at what actually happened than what we could have ever hoped for.

The human knot activity, one that is used for developing leadership in the children and in workplaces across the world, is one of the more simple activities that is a part of the 2+2=5 program. In the last several years of operating this program, facilitators have run the Human Knot probably hundreds of times, always expecting similar results as years before.

One day, while running the Human Knot, I came across an occurrence that ultimately *changed my life.* If all other days of running this program had been a *complete* failure, and I still had this one particular day, it would have all been worth it.

Jenny was a fourth grade student who I met in the first year of running the 2+2=5 program. I have never before and never again come across such a unique individual. The first time I met her, I thought that I must have done something wrong. She completely avoided eye contact with me, never even said hi or responded to my questions, and rarely ever participated in the 2+2=5 activities.

She would usually pull herself away from the activity within minutes. Other times, she simply would not even start the activity at all. I would usually see her sitting in the corner of the gym, undoubtedly counting down the minutes until physical education class was over.

I became a little concerned because all of the other children seemed to be really enjoying the 2+2=5 program. I would constantly try to visit her and get her involved in the 2+2=5 activities; but she never spoke a word to me or any of the other college facilitators.

Until one day, Jenny's principal called me into her office for a meeting to discuss Jenny's behavior and her lack of participation in the program. The principal told me, Jenny, whose name has been changed to protect the confidentiality of the child, was a selective mute.

I had never heard of such a thing and asked for any more information that she could provide. Her principal explained that she was a selective mute and would not speak to adults at all, except for her parents. She wouldn't speak to her teachers, not one word. If a teacher called on her in class, she would tell the answer to the person sitting next to her and that person would relay the answer. If she had to make a presentation to the class, she would record it at home and give the tape to the teacher. She wouldn't speak to her teachers and she certainly didn't speak to any of the college 2+2=5 facilitators. To my knowledge, she had never spoken a word to an adult other than her parents.

During the first six weeks of running the 2+2=5 program, there was not one positive development with Jenny. Until one perfect day, the college facilitators were performing the Human Knot activity during the leadership lesson. The team children was all in a tangled mass as each child was screaming over all of the others, trying to shout out instructions to the rest of the team; no one was listening to anyone else. As expected, Jenny was on the sidelines, watching, once again unwilling to speak or interact.

As the children continue to struggle through the Human Knot, I saw Jenny out of the corner of my eye, marching over to the Human Knot. Jenny tapped me on the wrist and screamed out to me, "This is never going to work!"

LEADERSHIP

.I asked her why. She replied, "No one's listening!!! Everyone's screaming and no one's listening."

And now I was the speechless one.

I was shocked that she finally spoke to us, but not nearly as shocked as her teacher. The team decided to choose one person who was allowed to talk and the rest of the team could not speak, only listen. In a truly awesome moment, the team chose Jenny to lead them and to be the only speaker. Jenny directed the team to untangle the human knot and the team was ultimately successful climaxing with loud cheers and applause.

The smile on Jenny's face was worth more than anything. In the remaining four weeks of the program, Jenny continued to participate in each of the activities by taking on a bigger role in the team activities and being involved in more and more discussion with the college facilitators. It was truly remarkable. I have had the opportunity to be around many inspirational and moving leaders in my career but that day, Jenny taught me how to be an inspirational leader and how to command the attention and respect of the team. She was the unexpected leader and she rose to an incredible height that day. Leaders draw internal strength during difficult tasks and rise to the level necessary to be successful.

Several months later, I revisited the elementary school where I met with the principal once again. Not surprisingly, she told me that Jenny had continued to make incredible strides. She was now talking to her teachers in class regularly and had gained immeasurable confidence in herself. She was getting better grades in all of her classes because of the exuberating level of confidence in herself, and she was interacting more with her peers. She was happy and to be quite honest, an entirely different person.

As the 2+2=5 program works with fourth and fifth graders, Jenny participated in the program again as a fifth grader. The second year was night and day to the first year. Jenny was actively participated in all of the activities and assuming leadership roles on her team without reserve.

You see, I always thought the human knot activity was a little hokey or cheesy, and under-estimated the potential impact of the human knot activity. It's a great activity, but it doesn't seem necessarily glamorous compared to some of the other 2+2=5 activities. As managers, we take the opportunity to run these or similar activities in order to foster leadership in our teams. We do these activities because we may be completely surprised by who rises to the occasion when given the opportunity to demonstrate situational leadership.

Roger, a fifth grade student concluded, "A leader is not a boss. A leader always puts the team before themselves. No matter what, they keep the team goal in mind and listen to the team members." Right on, Roger. I've read so many leadership books on the market; and I don't hesitate to say that I learned more about leadership from a couple of fourth graders than I ever did from an entire stack of leadership books. Leadership is not a position on a team; it is a quality of a team. A team that values effective leadership may have a different leader on any given day, depending on the situation that the team finds itself in. This is known as situational leadership.

A couple of ten year-olds taught me that leadership is neither a position head on a team nor is leadership a title. Leadership is a quality that is found on a team.

How do managers develop leadership skills on their team? Leadership can be developed simply by giving team members an opportunity to demonstrate leadership and develop confidence in their leadership skills. No textbook or training can possibly teach someone to be a true leader. We don't truly know and understand effective leadership until it hits us square between the eyes and we are forced to carry the torch for our team. Then as leaders, we draw upon inner strength and move forward into the role as team leader.

It's simple. How we lead others typically reflects how we like to be led. The children were able to make observations about how their classmates were leading their teams and then either used those techniques or modify them as to what they think would work as an effective team leader. Until we are presented with the opportunity to lead a team, we don't really know how we would respond to the call of leadership. It is a manager's responsibility to prepare their team members for their opportunity to lead by allowing team members to explore situational leadership.

CHAPTER FIVE

ESSENTIAL DIVERSITY

"Diversity is important. He thinks different than me. If we hadn't had each other's ideas, we would have never finished the activity." **- Sheila, fourth grade**

As our workplaces become more and more diverse, managers have started to appreciate, more deeply, the value and the need for diversity on a work team. Few would argue the fact that diversity of any fashion typically yields diversity of thought which should be considered invaluable in teambuilding. In addition, although recognizing the benefit, few would argue that diversity of thought often puts additional strain on teams and their managers. Therefore, so much emphasis has been placed around managing diversity and the importance of being able to leverage the strength that diversity brings to a team atmosphere. Diversity can easily be one of the greatest strengths or greatest weaknesses of a team based on the team management's ability to leverage the benefits of diversity.

A Day in the Office

Bob is the manager at a Nebraskan retail store. He has rarely been exposed to people that are different than him. Bob is trying to explore adding a new product line to the retail store and is having trouble with making

ESSENTIAL DIVERSITY

the decision as to add the product line or not. Yi, who works at the retail store as a sales associate, is Chinese, and volunteered to help with the special project. At the first project meeting, Bob announced that the team had to put together some prospective financial statements for investors. He said, "Yi, could you try to figure that out? You must be good with math."

When our brains try to quickly process information about people, we automatically search our internal database to tell us as much as we can about someone based on their outward appearance. Many of these assumptions or stereotypes are often wrong; however, it is a natural process that our brain uses as a shortcut to tell us what we think we know about someone. These stereotypes are not only socially inappropriate; they can often act as barriers to the team success. Individuals on the team are unique in their abilities. Managers who put people into buckets based on stereotypes are under leveraging the strengths of the individuals on the team.

Discussing diversity as professional managers is challenging enough; try discussing diversity with a bunch of fourth and fifth graders. Surprisingly, the children had some interesting things to say about the importance of diversity and what that asset contributes to the success of a team. The children boiled down a complex topic into its simplest terms and arrived at a new sense of appreciation for the value of diversity on a team. The 2+2=5 program uses two activities to approach the concept of diversity. Managers can use these activities to foster an understanding and appreciation for team diversity.

Labeling Activity

The facilitator provides a package of various stickers. Each of the sticker labels has a different shape. Some of the stickers have triangles, some have circles, some squares and so on. Some have designs; some are one color, different colors and so on. Some of the stickers have no similarity to any other sticker in the room. No one in the room is placed on a team to begin the activity. The facilitator instructs the room to maintain silence throughout the activity. Then, the facilitator places one sticker on each individual's back without allowing the individual to see the sticker. Then the facilitator asks the crowd to put themselves in appropriate teams without speaking.

The individuals will then attempt to communicate non-verbally (using hand signals etc.) in order to put themselves into teams based on the sticker on each other's back. The facilitator will observe the behavior of accepting/rejecting based on a label. Once everyone has agreed that they are in an "appropriate" team, or upon a designated time limit, the activity has ended. A discussion about diversity and the impact of labeling on a group of people then occurs.[6]

Please note, the facilitator does not specifically instruct the individuals to use the stickers. It is the facilitator's responsibility to ask the question of primary importance, "Why did you use the labels to put yourselves into teams?"

---

[6] Adapted from Massachusetts Campus Compact, November 2003.

It is important to leverage the reflection to discuss how we use labels to make decisions about people each day. The discussion should include developing an understanding about why we use labels and how we can be more conscious of this in everyday life.

Reflection Questions: Please note that the following questions can be used by the facilitator to help lead the reflection discussion after the activity is completed. Facilitators can use these questions or other questions generated as a result of the observations from the activity.

- Why do you think we have a tendency of identifying people by their visible labels?
- What qualities do we decipher on others' labels more quickly?
- Discuss some of the advantages of a highly diverse team?
- What does this activity tell us about diversity and our natural response to diversity?
- How can we use diversity to make our teams more effective and successful?
- Why did you automatically assume that the labels were the right way to get into our work teams when you weren't instructed to use the labels?

Picture Link Activity

Each team receives an envelope of 50 clipart cards. The team is responsible for linking the pictures together by way of connecting last letter of one word to first letter of the next word. For example, a picture of lips connects to stapler by way of the "s". Then a picture of a rock connects to the end of stapler and so on. The objective is to link as many pictures together as possible. The team with the longest chain, in a limited time period, is the winner.

Dynamics involved with this activity very much revolve around diversity. People of different backgrounds will see and describe certain pictures differently than others. It will be essential to consider all points of view on the team in order to maximize the potential for picture linkage.

Reflection Questions: Please note that the following questions can be used by the facilitator to help lead the reflection discussion after the activity is completed. Facilitators can use these questions or other questions generated as a result of the observations from the activity.

- How does a team's diversity impact the success of the team in this activity? How does diversity impact the team environment in other situations at work?
- What challenge does diversity present in teamwork?
- What does this activity teach us about the link between effective communication and problem solving for

teams?
- Describe your team's strategic approach to this activity. What elements did you find to be effective?

Diversity and Emotion

In week seven, as facilitators, we decided to address the need to recognize diversity and its importance to teams. The college facilitators did some preliminary research about the demographics of the elementary schools before beginning the activity. According to greatschools.net, which provides academic, socioeconomic, and ethnicity figures for most elementary schools, this particular elementary school is reported as 86% white.

In my experience with facilitating the 2+2=5 program at this particular elementary school, it appeared that a vast majority of the student population was homogenous from a diversity perspective. In particular, it was important to discuss the role of diversity in teams, especially for these particular classes. I expected the children to struggle with the activity because most of the students did not have exposure to a wide degree of diversity. What I didn't expect, however, was the level of emotion that went along with the activity that we worked on for that particular week.

The activity, called 'Labeling' involved addressing how we use labels to identify and classify each other and how people tend to put people in groups or classifications based on one or two outward characteristics. As I briefed the class on the importance of diversity for teams, my co-facilitator placed a label on the back of each student. These labels each had a shape on it with various patterns or colors. Some people had stickers with circles, squares, or triangles and with various colors. Then the students were instructed to put themselves into a team, without talking.

The students in the class began the activity by scrambling to look at all of the other students' labels. The students used gestures to communicate what shape the student had on their back. Some students pointed to different colored objects to communicate the color of the shape. While other students, noticeably leaders, were actually dragging some students into groups that had similar shapes. Some of the children were using color as an identifying characteristic, while others were using the shape as the identifying characteristic as to how they were separating into teams based on the stickers.

Then, unexpectedly, the emotion kicked in. Before beginning the activity, I intentionally prepared the labels such that two students would have labels with shapes and patterns that did not logically fall into any particular group. These two students, walked back and forth between clusters of people as a majority of the students were now finding teams with which to identify. These two children would turn their back towards the teams that were forming, hoping for the team members to wave them into the team. Cluster after cluster, the student, Kevin, turned to show his label and was promptly rejected by the group. It became obvious that he was feeling the pressure of putting himself into a team and the frustration of failing to find acceptance. Each time he approached a team, he was told, through gestures, that he didn't belong. Even one particular student, Sarah, the leader of the class, who was trying to help put Kevin into a group, was feeling the pressure. It was obvious that frustration continued to mount as I announced that there was only one minute remaining to join a group that they were sure they belonged to. Kevin continued to run back and forth looking at the labels around the class, each time finding people that were pushing him away from their team.

Finally, the time expired, leaving Kevin in the middle of the gym without a group to identify with the label on his back. I asked the class an obvious question, "How did you decide to break down into teams?" The students answered that they used the shapes on the labels to divide the teams. The students began talking about how they used their hands to describe to others what the sticker was on their back. I further asked them, "Why did you decide to use the labels?"

After no response, I said, "The directions were to put yourself into a team. I didn't say that you had to use a label. I said put yourself in a team that you belong to. Why did anyone even move from their spot? Isn't this class one team?" We then broke down the process of finding a team to belong to and how diversity impacts a team environment. Clearly, the children assumed that they were supposed to use the labels. More importantly, it was interesting to consider why our first instinct was to use the labels to put people into teams. This activity was an interesting experiment which fairly represents the diverse situations found in our work environments. Without the presence of a sticker, many of us use other outward characteristics as identifiers to help put each other into teams or cliques.

Another interesting question remained, as Kevin stood in the middle of the gym, still not part of a team. I asked Kevin, "How did it feel to not be able to find a group and how did it feel to be rejected by the other teams?" He answered, simply and accurately, "It was terrible. I was mad at them and mad at myself."

The facilitator asked the other members of the class to think about how they would feel if they couldn't find a team or group to fit in with and how it might feel to be rejected based on a label. Without being conscious of the event, Kevin was becoming self-aware and the rest of the class was empathizing with his experience. Some students began to act and feel how Kevin felt. The students were left wondering why they formed groups according to one outward characteristic, the label. Fitting perfectly into the lesson about diversity, I asked the class, "How did it feel to be accepted or rejected based upon a label that you had no control over? The facilitators put a label on your back at the beginning of the class and you had no choice what it would look like." The children responded that it wasn't fair to be judged by the label, but that it was their first instinct for putting each other into teams.

In what seemed to be a rarely perfect learning opportunity, the children taught the facilitators to think about how it felt to be labeled by others, rejected or accepted based on our label, and then related the experience to diversity in the world, both inside and outside of the classroom. Finally, the children taught us to understand that diversity on a team is critical because the different points of view come into play based on varying backgrounds. The transfer of contagious emotions between the class and the empathy that was developed in nearly the entire class brought about one of the most excellent learning opportunities throughout the entire 2+2=5 program.

Team Thought and Groupthink

When teams are made up of generally homogeneous team members, growing up in the same schools, with the same cultural background, the same family life, the same values and the same social construct, teams are generally less productive, less effective, and less successful. Diversity on a team helps with team brainstorming and problem solving. When people look at a problem differently, the range of solutions tends to expand, allowing a team to find the best, most effective solution to a problem. Often times, as homogeneous team members, when one team member offers a solution that falls within our expected solution set, we fail to challenge the team to find solutions outside of our expectation set. In more simple terms, we fail to think outside the box.

Groupthink is defined by Webster's dictionary as "a pattern of thought characterized by self-deception, forced manufacture of consent, and conformity to group values and ethics." When we have diversity on a team, there is a better likelihood of beating groupthink because of the diverse range in thought. During a diversity session, Colleen made this comment about why it is important to have diversity on a team, "Because if you all think the same thing, you might think you have a good plan, but it might be a bad plan and someone who knows different things could point that out." Colleen was eluding that diversity causes a variety of thinking.

Catherine, age ten, added, "(If there was diversity on a team) there would be a lot of different ideas that the team could join together to help them succeed. If one group was made up of a bunch of the same people, there would probably be a lack of ideas because we are the same. Everyone works differently. When there's diversity in a team, it's good because it brings a lot of different ideas to the table."

Gender and Diversity

We often think of diversity as racial and ethnic diversity, but it is also important to think of diversity in terms of men and women: gender diversity. Any parent of a nine or ten year-old, knows that boys and girls think of each other as cooties! When the boys and girls were helping each other get into teams based on the sticker on their back without talking, Will, age twelve, made this gender observation: "Girls guided people to the team that matched their sticker and boys tried to explain what the sticker was." While this quote does not exactly provide reliable insight into the way boys and girls lead teams differently, it is still striking that a fourth grader was able to pick up on the fact that boys and girls interact and lead team members differently. Rebecca said, "I would have a lot more fun in this game if my team was all girls, but we definitely wouldn't have won without having boys and girls on the team."

ESSENTIAL DIVERSITY

Needless to say, there have been far more sophisticated studies done on gender diversity than simply observing a room of fourth graders; however, these fourth graders were able to demonstrate that men and women think and interact differently. The bottom line is we are different. High performing teams are able to leverage those differences to strengthen the team. Effective teams go out of their way to leverage those differences to find success, to be high performing. Recognizing that we are different, we can begin to understand those differences and what strengths each individual possesses. A true, high performing team leverages the personal strengths of each individual on the team. Shannon, age eleven, concluded, "It is important to have many roles on a team so you can help each other and you can stay organized and know that everybody has different strengths. We have to understand them and use them."

Diversity and Communication

When we are in diverse situations, it is of utmost importance to consider the way we communicate and the possibility that we are offensive to others who may be different than us. Who better to demonstrate unwitting offense than a ten year-old? Brian goes to a primarily white, affluent elementary school. Talisha is a freshman college student. Talisha is about to take part in her first 2+2=5 session as a coach. She is meeting with her team and asking them about their names and interests, when Brian, age ten, blurts out, "I like you. You look like someone I know!"

"Oh that's nice," Talisha chimes back.

"Ya, you look a lot like my maid," Brian answers back, straight-faced, not having any idea what he had just said. It was clear to everyone that he did not mean to hurt Talisha. He clearly did not have any idea how offensive his comment was, although it was evident that Talisha was hurt by his comments.

Talisha, clearly upset, left the team and the physical education gymnasium and didn't come back for over fifteen minutes. The occurrence happened unbeknownst to me. I had not heard of its happening until we discussed it in the car on the ride back from the 2+2=5 session. Talisha had clearly gotten over the incident, but wanted to discuss more deeply the underlying societal problems that surrounded this occurrence. For the following week's session, I received notice from Talisha that she was upset that she couldn't go to the elementary school because she had become very sick.

Within minutes of the second week's teambuilding session, Brian approached me and said, "Where's Talisha? What happened? Is she coming back?"

I told him that she was sick and that she would be back next week. Although he didn't say anything else about what happened the week before, I could sense a tiny bit of guilt running through Brian's voice as he asked about Talisha. It was becoming obvious that Brian had thought about what he had said and had realized it was wrong.

The next week came, and Talisha was back in the gym for another 2+2=5 session. Brian avoided her for approximately the first twenty minutes. Finally, he approached her saying, "Why weren't you here last week? Scott said you were sick. Were you? I probably shouldn't have said that you were like my maid. I'm sorry if what I said made you sad."

If a fourth grader can realize that what he said was wrong and admits to it, why can't a board room of executives? Truthfully, we have all said something at some point that was either intentionally or unintentionally offensive to a teammate. Being conscious of our social, cultural, ethnic, and racial differences helps us become more acutely aware of what we say, the impact that it could have on someone else, and its potential for offending someone. Communication plays a tremendously important role in the way we function as a team. We must be able to exercise empathy and put ourselves in the shoes of others in order to understand how our communication is perceived. Appreciation of diversity in a team culture is a function of a high performing team.

Making the Link

A team of fifth grade students huddled around the fifty clipart cards about ready to start the Picture Link activity. Each team had to connect the pictures together using the last letter of the first word and the first letter of the next word. For example, a picture of lips logically link to a picture of a snake because of the shared "s" and subsequently snake links to eagle because of the shared "e". The objective of the activity is to create the longest chain link of clipart as possible. The real challenge of the activity is to think of alternate names for the clipart. For example, if someone was trying to link the eagle card but didn't have another "e", you might suggest calling the picture "bird" instead to try to link using the "b" and the "d".

In six years of running the 2+2=5 program, I have found that without a doubt, far and away, the most successful teams to complete this activity had a strong mix of diversity and background. Our cultural and ethnic backgrounds provide us with a stored bank of information that we use all the time in decision making or, even more simply, how we see the world. When we see a piece of clipart, we quickly search our internal database of information in order to determine what we would call that particular image, what word we associate with that particular image. Teams with diverse backgrounds have a wider variety of stored information and are more likely to be successful at the Picture Link activity.

Take for example, ten year-old Grady, who had just transferred to this Massachusetts elementary school from the Midwest. There was a picture of a grocery bag on one of the clipart pictures. The team was shouting out bag, groceries, food, but none of it successfully linked to the end of the previous clipart picture. Until after a couple minutes, Grady, said "That's not a bag, that's a sack." The team stopped and looked at him as if he had three heads, unsure of why he would call the picture a "sack". Then Grady explained that back home they called it a sack, not a bag. The team switched the card to "sack" and continued the link. Grady used a word that only he had stored in his internal database. That moment demonstrated the value of diverse thought on a team and its key to team success.

Of course, I am not the first one to say that diversity impacts the way we see the world and that diversity is an asset for teams. I think, for the most part, it is a pretty basic and universally accepted idea; but, a team of fourth graders taught me how valuable diversity of thought is to a team. Inarguably, we all look at the world through our different lenses. We can leverage those differences by being conscious of each other's strengths and considering the need for diversity when building our work teams. This doesn't necessarily mean that we need just diversity of race, culture, or ethnicity, but also leveraging any other differences that we may have. Think about other difference that we have in the workplace and build a team that leverages those differences as opposed to selecting teammates that are homogenous in nature. Even just as simple as building a work team with someone from the marketing department, someone from the finance department, someone from sales, someone from management, and someone from manufacturing; each person will have a different view of how to solve a problem and a different view of the company as a whole.

CHAPTER SIX

PROBLEM SOLVING

"First, everybody thought of an idea, we brainstormed and then decided on the best plan. Our strategy was to work together and help each other."
– Samantha, fifth grade

Teams are put together to solve problems, period. One way or another, regardless of a team's goals, purpose, objectives, or mission, teams solve problems. Every team works towards solving problems every day. Problem solving is very much about success and failure, winning and losing; however, that does not paint the whole picture. How efficiently or effectively we solve problems, as a team, dictates the long-term success of a team. Even if we win in the short term, we may be losing in the long term because of the way our team solves problems.

A Day in the Office

Imagine you are on an audit team with a very large firm and you're working on one of the firm's biggest clients. Here lies the problem: the audit must be completed by March 31st. You have a team of seven employees and there's three weeks left to complete the

PROBLEM SOLVING

audit. Each person is working solely on his or her individual task.

To begin with, the audit team did not have a reasonable, workable, realistic strategy in place before starting the audit. As the weeks rolled by, on the four month long project, the team was slowly falling behind the unrealistic schedule that was set out at the beginning of the audit. The original strategic plan did not foresee or consider some of the setbacks that occurred during the audit and this had set the team off schedule significantly.

In the closing weeks, each member the audit team worked tirelessly for 100 hours a week for three weeks straight, clearly lacking sleep, any semblance of a personal life, and was at the breaking point. The audit completion wraps up on March 31st at 11:00 PM, just before the deadline. Fortunately, the audit has been completed and the goal of the team has been reached. However, after the project reaches completion, five of the seven team members quit the firm.

The audit team succeeded in completing the goal it had set out by the deadline, but at what cost? The team was completely destroyed for the long-term because of the way the team managed its task. The way in which teams go about solving problems definitely has a direct impact on a team's long-term success. Teams that most effectively solve problems, exercise and develop their problem solving skills on a regular basis. Managers can build their team's effective problem solving processes by using the following team building activities:

Ball Craze Activity

The facilitator will arrange four hula hoops at each corner of the room/activity field and one hula hoop in the middle. Place 50-75 balls (tennis size) in the middle hula hoop. Divide into four teams.

The object of the game is for each team to get all of the tennis balls in its own corner hoop. Once you have all of the balls within your hoop, you win. As a rule, there is no throwing or tossing of the balls. In addition, no one person can be holding or carrying more than one ball at a time. All the balls must be out of the middle before the students can take from other hoops. There is no defending the hoops so teams must allow other teams to be able to steal balls from the other teams' hoops.

Facilitator Note: Play will go on for about five to ten minutes of the team members running back and forth between hoops, transferring tennis balls with little to no net gain in the teams' tennis ball total. At the pause in the game, the facilitator should ask the teams to stop for two minutes to evaluate and adjust their strategy. Then after another five minutes of play, ask the teams to regroup again and re-evaluate the strategy.

After awhile the team will reconsider the goal and hopefully the teams will recognize that they are able to move the hoops. As the activity continues, the team members should ultimately realize that the only way to win in this activity is for everyone to win. (The solution is for all of the teams to place all of the balls in the middle hoop and each team is to put their team hoop around it.)

PROBLEM SOLVING

Facilitator note: Ultimately, the activity challenges teams to solve problems using "out of the box thinking." Participants will begin to consider the importance of work teams as working towards a common goal, such as increased profitability, rather than working against each other in a more cutthroat environment. This challenges people to realize that teams don't always work against each other; sometimes multiple teams have the appearance that they are competing but are actually working towards a shared common goal.

Reflection Questions: Please note that the following questions can be used by the facilitator to help lead the reflection discussion after the activity is completed. Facilitators can use these questions or other questions generated as a result of the observations from the activity.

- Describe the frustration on the team when it was discovered that your strategy would not be successful. What did you do then?
- How did the frustration impact the dynamic of the team during the activity?
- This activity represents a model of multiple teams working towards a unified goal rather than working against each other. Where else can this be applied in our organization?
- Discuss the importance of adapting and modifying strategy as the activity progresses.
- In what ways can we become better problem solvers after having experienced this activity?

The Flying Egg Activity

The facilitator will provide each team with the following materials: twenty five drinking straws, twenty toothpicks, twenty feet of masking tape, twenty feet of scotch tape, twenty feet of string, one square yard of tissue paper, and one egg. Depending on the preference of the facilitator, the provided materials may be adjusted to vary the difficulty of the activity.

The facilitator will inform the teams that they have some resources to complete the challenge of building a device that will protect the team's egg when dropped from approximately eight feet high. The container dimensions must not exceed one foot by one foot by one foot. Containers can be made using only the materials provided. The container must have a hatch or a door. Any team that violates these regulations will be disqualified. The facilitator can modify these rules in order to adjust the difficulty of the activity depending on the age level of the participants. After the time limit is up, teams will use their contraption to drop the egg. Teams who are able to drop their egg without it breaking have succeeded in this activity.

Reflection Questions: Please note that the following questions can be used by the facilitator to help lead the reflection discussion after the activity is completed. Facilitators can use these questions or other questions generated as a result of the observations from the activity.

PROBLEM SOLVING

- Describe the process used by your team for solving the Flying Egg problem.
- What elements of the strategic process were particularly effective?
- What does this activity teach us about effective problem solving?
- What areas of our life would these skills be useful and important? How about in our organization?
- Describe the effectiveness and efficiency of your team's use of resources.
- In what ways could your team have better managed its resources?
- How did resource management and the limited extent of resources impact the team dynamic?

Strategize

Over 3,000 fourth and fifth graders have been through the 2+2=5 program. Not a single team began an activity by developing a strategy before jumping in first. No sooner does the facilitator begin explaining the instructions than do the children dive headfirst into the activity's materials, often being wasteful of their resources. One of the biggest wastes of resources of course was time.

That is, of course, until week eight of the program, when the facilitators teach the lesson of "problem solving." When we get into a new project, we can be often overcome with emotions: excitement, enthusiasm, frustration, or discouragement. These emotions often get in the way of clear, rationale thought, which would tell us that it is logical and reasonable to form a strategy before beginning to solve a problem or complete a task.

Sometimes we are under such a time crunch to complete the project that we forgo strategizing in order to "save" time or what we perceive as saving time. Forgoing strategizing is typically a time cost rather than a time saver and responsible, high performing teams recognize the benefit of strategizing. Leah, a fourth grader, said "We only had twenty minutes to finish the project, we were all in a rush, but we had to talk about it first so everyone else wouldn't be doing something different."

The act of merely strategizing is not the be all and end all of problem solving. Teams must not only strategize, but strategize effectively in order to identify solutions that they might not have thought of had they recklessly jumped into the activity.

PROBLEM SOLVING

The fourth grade teams dumped out their "Flying Egg" materials on the floor. I've seen thousands of children make a wide variety of contraptions for the flying egg, each one being unique.

This particular session began as any other, as the children eagerly and immediately started to form a parachute. Then Gretchen said, "Wait, let's think about this. Is there anything else that we could make?" The team paused and looked at her and put down the supplies. Then, other members of the team began to suggest alternatives. After a short strategizing session, the team came up with something that I had never seen before. They decided to use their resources to develop a landing pad for the egg, rather than build a contraption to drop the egg with. That particular day, they were the only team to succeed with the Flying Egg activity. It was unconventional, and certainly unexpected, but it was successful and the team would have never arrived at such a solution without a team member challenging the team to take an extra moment to devote to strategizing.

While facilitating the 2+2=5 program, teams of fourth and fifth graders taught me that there are at least three keys to effective strategizing.

Understand and Evaluate Resources

First, the team must understand the extent of its resources before the team begins its task. This includes not only physical resources, but also intangible resources. Teams must evaluate its human resources by understanding the strengths and capabilities of the individual team members. In addition, teams must assess resources, such as time, and plan a reasonable goal-oriented deadline with specific milestones. "Setting our goal was hard, we wanted our team to be focused," said Megan in the fifth grade. Consider the audit team mentioned earlier. Their strategy for audit completion was unrealistic. Strategic plans must be aggressive enough to get the team to stretch but not so aggressive that they are seen to be unattainable. Setting unattainable goals only serves to discourage the team.

A team of fifth graders was about to embark on the "Flying Egg" activity. The team had a finite set of resources: twenty five drinking straws, twenty toothpicks, twenty feet of masking tape, twenty feet of scotch tape, twenty feet of string, one sheet (one square yard) of tissue paper, and one egg. Ben and Zoe, fifth graders, tore open the bag of supplies and immediately began taping toothpicks to the border of the tissue paper. Zoe took the straws and started taping them together in a long line. Rebecca, the leader of the team, began to draw out a plan on a sheet of paper with the help of two other team members. The team planned to build a parachute contraption with a basket hanging below the parachute, similar to a hot air balloon. When Rebecca and the two other team members finished their strategy, they realized Ben and Zoe have already cost the team half of its supplies. Rebecca tore the tissue paper out of Ben's hand, literally tearing the paper. Sure, let's attribute this to the immaturity of a few fifth graders, but how many of us can say that this happens in their workplace almost everyday? I know that it has happened nearly everyday in the places that I have worked. How often do we receive an

PROBLEM SOLVING

email with team instructions and begin working on a project before the work team has even had a chance to meet for the first time?

As the activity continued, it became clear that Rebecca's strategy was not going to work. Ben says, "You should have taken my idea. You didn't listen to my idea." Ben never participated in the strategy and brainstorming; he just jumped right in, failing to contribute to the formulation of a strategic plan.

Strategize, Evaluate, Re-strategize

Forming an initial strategy is not even half the battle. Try and think about the last time you were on a team in which the team's initial strategy worked 100% to plan, right through completion of the project. Teams must constantly evaluate its progress and re-strategize as unexpected variables arise. The ability to stop and take stock of the team's progress and re-evaluate the strategy is critical to team problem solving.

"We had a plan, it didn't work, so we had to change the plan. I don't see why we even made a plan in the first place," Silvia, age ten, said.

"Think about it Silvia, if we didn't have a plan first, we would have been totally lost about how to make it work. We would have wasted so much time to start," Mike replied.

When Rebecca realized that the team's egg flying strategy was not going to work, she made the entire team stop and take inventory of the remaining resources. "Everyone stop! What do we have left to get this done?" Rebecca said. The team re-evaluated its resources and updated their strategy to see how they could make it work.

Think Bigger!
 The need to re-evaluate team strategy is never more crucial in the 2+2=5 program than with the Ball Craze activity, one of the most challenging 2+2=5 activities. The class is divided into four teams. By establishing four teams, the children have the initial perception that the teams are working against each other to gather the tennis balls into their team's hula hoop. Upon more careful re-evaluation, the team reconsiders the instructions and updates its strategy.

 The activity typically lasts about one hour to complete, but really only takes about five seconds to complete if the team finds the correct solution. However, of course no team has ever come up with the solution right away. Each session of Ball Craze starts the same way. Children run back and forth carrying tennis balls back to their team's hula hoop while members of other teams are stealing balls from their hoop. Imagine twenty five fourth and fifth graders running back and forth across the gym, stealing and being stolen from, with little to no net gain in tennis balls in their own hula hoop.

 After about thirty to forty minutes of running back and forth, one of the teams remembers that the facilitator instructed everyone to remember to revaluate the initial strategy. Finally, after about a half hour into the activity, the team huddles and decides to concentrate its efforts on stealing the balls from the closest hula hoop. The entire team attacks another team's hoop. The four

PROBLEM SOLVING

team members are now working together more efficiently but still resulting in little to no progress of tennis ball accumulation as the other teams steal back their tennis balls one by one.

Soon after, the team realizes that this strategy will not work because they know that they cannot win without having all of the tennis balls within their hoop. After about forty five minutes, the team re-huddles and decides to send a spokesperson/negotiator over to another team. Two of the four teams gather together to make an agreement not to steal tennis balls from each other. The teams agree to take tennis balls only from the other two teams. Quickly, the remaining two teams follow suit and join together.

Within another five minutes of running back and forth across the gym floor, the facilitator reminds the teams that in order to win, all of the tennis balls must be within your team's hula hoop. After six years of running the 2+2=5 program, inevitably, the fifty five to sixty minute point marks the final turning point in the activity. Finally, after nearly an hour, the teams realize that no team wins unless they all win. All of the balls are returned to the center, while each team moves its hula hoop over the center ring, and finally, everyone wins.

Where have we seen this "ball craze" in our everyday lives? Every company across the world has its own "ball craze". Each company has many different work teams each responsible for a specific project or goal. However, ultimately, each team is working towards the underlying main goal of company profitability and productivity. In the workplace, work teams can be so focused on their own specific team goal that we sabotage other teams or they steal other teams' resources, their "tennis balls." While it may help us accumulate our tennis balls, we are ultimately undermining the big picture goal of the entire company. Senior management is responsible for ensuring that work teams understand their role in the big picture. Just as we must think beyond our own individual responsibilities to focus on the team goal, we must also think beyond our own team's project to bring into focus the big picture goal. It is often effective and realistic to set milestones in task management, but we must always keep in mind the end goal and how it fits into the overall strategy.

Try and imagine giving a team of fourth graders a bag full of supplies to make an egg fly. Then try and imagine a scenario where the children wouldn't jump right in with the supplies, but would actually stop and make a strategy before starting. Ask any fourth grade teacher, it never happens. That's a 2+2=5 moment and it can happen for your company. Mandy, age eleven, concluded, "The most smartest thing I learned is that we have to plan, plan, plan! It would be impossible to build a bridge without planning first." And little did she know, that was exactly what she was about to do next...

CHAPTER SEVEN

NEGOTIATION

"A compromise is a negotiation where each person gets a little bit of what they want. Teams must be able to compromise with other teams and on our own team." – Tony, age twelve.

Try to remember the last time you negotiated on a team. Were you successful? How do you define a successful negotiation? Were you comfortable? Were you nervous? How about the other person? Did they seem more comfortable than you? Did both parties get what they wanted or have to give up a little to make it work? What were you thinking and feeling?

My dad always told me, "Help other people get what they want and you will see that ultimately you will get what you want." This is some fine advice to live by, but you might argue that the art of effective negotiation is even more sophisticated. It is so sophisticated, in fact, that I learned everything I know about negotiation from a ten year-old!

When I think about negotiation skills, I'm constantly drawing back to this case study that I completed in a college negotiation class.[7] It was a two person partner

---
[7] Ugli Organge Negotiation Case

NEGOTIATION

exercise; each person has one of the two roles specified in the case study. Each of you received your role card which outlined what you wanted and your motivations for why you wanted it. Each person could read their own role card but had no idea what the other person wanted or why they wanted it. Each person played the part of a scientist and each was working on a cure for a new medicine: one person was working on a medicine that cured asthma and one that cured a very rare but deadly disease.

Each scientist needed the entire worldwide crop of oranges to make the medicine. As you both sat there and debated the other person about the merits of curing one disease or the other, or negotiating who could financially outbid whom, each person failed to realize the clincher in the negotiation. The fact sheet of one scientist's role card, read "You need the orange peels from the entire crop." Whereas, in contrast, the other person's fact sheet read "You need the orange pulp from the entire crop."

Surely, this solution seems simple when it is put so plainly in front of your eyes: each person gets the piece they need from the orange crop. I assure you that we sat there for nearly an hour arguing about the societal impact of choosing to curing asthma versus a rare but deadly disease. Neither one of us was so inclined to clarify what the other person needed. When we stumbled across the solution, of course we felt foolish, but I wondered, what would a fourth grader have done in this situation?

A Day in the Office

Imagine you are on a team that is writing a beta version of some new software about to hit the market. You have some of the best programmers in the world working on your team. Unfortunately, you hit a speed bump in the design and implementation of the new software. Your team of programmers can't seem to wrap its head around some of the usability problems that users have been expressing in focus groups.

All of your team members are more than technically competent but are missing the picture from the end user. You decide to negotiate for a person's time from another team who is already working on another project. The other team has a team member who has tremendous experience in this area as well as a unique ability to interpret and clarify these "usability problems". This team looked outside of its limited resources to see what resource it could negotiate for from another team.

Does this sound like it happens in your workplace? It may happen, it may not, but chances are it doesn't happen one hundred percent of the time. More often than not, teams have such tunnel vision on their particular project that the team fails to evaluate the other potential resources it has outside of the core team and core resources. We are so focused internally on the team project that we fail to look outside of the team. How about a team of fourth graders? How would they do?

Have you ever found yourself in a situation where you had to negotiate with another team or even amongst your own team members? We negotiate every day. Most of the time, we don't even realize that we are negotiating, even as we are doing it. Understanding how to negotiate effectively and being conscious of how we are negotiating helps us more easily create team success. Managers can exercise their team's negotiation skills using the following activities.

Building Bridges Activity

The facilitator provides each team with one newspaper and approximately ten feet of masking tape. Each team is instructed as follows: Your team has been hired by ABC Engineering Company to develop a prototype of a new bridge that will be built in Southern California. They have provided each team with limited materials to design and build the most effective bridge. Additional resources may be negotiated with other teams (this is allowed but not explicitly announced in the directions to the teams). Here are the specifications of the prototype design:

Each bridge must be at least three feet long, one foot wide, and a height of ten inches. Failure to meet these specifications will result in disqualification. All qualifying bridges will be weight tested at the end of the construction time. The team whose bridge holds the most weight will be determined the winner. The facilitator will apply weight with books to the bridge and determine the winning team after twenty minutes of construction time. Resource variables, such as time allowed and tape/newspaper provided certainly can be manipulated in order to make the activity more or less difficult.

Reflection Questions: Please note that the following questions can be used by the facilitator to help lead the reflection discussion after the activity is completed. Facilitators can use these questions or other questions generated as a result of the observations from the activity.

- Did your team negotiate additional resources with another team? Were you successful in your negotiation? How could you have been more successful?
- How did you negotiate within your own team?
- What does this activity teach us about effective negotiation?
- Describe the negotiation dynamic within your team during the design phase of your strategy development. What strategies did you use to negotiate?
- How effectively and efficiently did your team utilize its limited resources?

Deserted Island Activity

The facilitator sets up the activity by telling the teams that they have just been stranded on a deserted island because they were on a plane that crashed over an uninhabited island. In fact, no one has ever lived on this island. Each team will receive a piece of poster sized paper with an outline of the island on it. The team will need to map out and diagram what they will develop on the island in order to survive. They should identify housing and other critical areas on the island map.

The facilitator notifies the team that they plane is still sinking into the ocean and there is a limited amount of time: five minutes with which to rescue some items from the plane. There is only enough time to rescue five items. The team members must choose which five items they would take with them from the plane before it sinks into the ocean. The items available in the plane include: first aid kit, matches, satellite radio, compass, map of the surrounding islands, ten gallons of water, tent, blankets, fifty feet of rope, flare gun, rifle, two suitcases (contents unknown), raft, and field survival book.

Generally, the facilitator can divide people into teams of four to five people. The team does not know what the other teams will choose to rescue. Other teams may choose different items and would provide opportunities for negotiation. If a team selects the suitcases, the facilitator will reveal the contents after selection.

The facilitator can also add a few resources that the team has with them. Then tell each team that there are a few other islands in the area that potentially have a different set of resources. Teams can arrange to trade or barter with the other islands, the other teams. Then have each team present their island and talk about what their priorities are for survival on the island and how they were able to come to an agreement about what to rescue.

Reflection Questions: Please note that the following questions can be used by the facilitator to help lead the reflection discussion after the activity is completed. Facilitators can use these questions or other questions generated as a result of the observations from the activity.

- How did your team arrive at the items selected from the plane?
- Describe how your team resolved differences in priority of items?
- What does this activity teach us about effective negotiation within our own team to arrive at the best possible solution?
- Did your team negotiate with other teams? What does this activity teach us about effective negotiations between different teams?
- How does communication impact the way we solve problems in the workplace?

Negotiating

When we negotiate, we are often negotiating for resources that we either need or want. For example, we may negotiate for more time to complete a project, a bigger budget for your department, a salary raise, or performance bonus. We are usually looking for more of *something*.

The fourth grade team sat down in the classroom, about to start on the "Building Bridges" activity. As a team, they were required to build a three foot long bridge out of limited resources of tape and newspaper. The team, whose bridge supports the most weight, is declared the activity winner. The facilitator's focus of the activity is on the team's intra-team negotiation skills and how the teammates negotiate with each other to solve the building bride activity.

Each team member, of this one particular fourth grade team, started pulling out supplies from the supply box. After having just received a lesson on the importance of strategizing, in the prior week, the team started designing the bridge it wanted to build by drawing it out on paper first.

The team then assigned each person on the team a specific role. "Johnny, you will be in charge of the base, Matty, you will be in charge of the length of the bridge. Samantha, you will be in charge of the resources. Make sure we don't use to much tape." I must tell you, watching this team work so successfully, out of the gate, and the way that they approached the task was truly a sight to see. They were perhaps one of the teams that had developed the most in their growth throughout the

NEGOTIATION

2+2=5 program. As a team, they were really putting the teambuilding principles to effective use.

Well, poor Samantha, who was in charge of the tape, got so caught up in helping to build the base of the bridge with Johnny, that she was giving out tape left and right to the team without really considering how much tape was left for the rest of the bridge. She was using it quite liberally and before long, the tape was completely gone. The state of the bridge was only about half done!

Each of the three boys started yelling at Samantha, "We told you to be careful with that, we told you, we told you! How could you run out of tape? How could you?!?" As one can imagine, Samantha began to cry, and begged me for more tape. Surely, there was no more tape to be had. I felt so bad for them that I wished I could have given them another ten feet of tape, but I couldn't.

Facilitators walk a fine line between effective coaching and giving away solutions. I took one look at that dilapidated bridge and I knew right then and there that the only chance they had was to start pulling some of the tape off and re-applying it to other areas. They were learning an important lesson about resource management. Surely, it was their only chance to finish building a bridge that would hold any weight at all.

That's when I saw Samantha get up and walk over to another team. What would be the first thing that would come to your mind as you are seeing this? I thought, "Oh no she's going to steal tape from another team." However, she began talking to her friend on the other team. I walked over to listen in on the conversation that went something like this...

"How's it going over here," Samantha interrupted.

"Eh, not so good. We have no chance to win; we ran out of newspaper," Nicole added.

"Ya, we ran out of tape. They're all blaming me but it's their own fault too. I didn't give them any tape unless they asked for it." Samantha said.

"I know. This game is stupid. There's not enough newspaper in this box to do this," Nicole screamed back.

And at that moment, the light bulb clicked in Samantha's mind. "Wait a minute, if you need newspaper, we could trade you some for some of your tape." And the deal went down in history as one of the shining moments of the 2+2=5 program.

The facilitator of the activity never mentioned that you could negotiate with other teams. In fact, at first, I thought I'd be looking to see how they would negotiate with each other on their own teams, such as who would complete what and how it would be completed. It took a fourth grader to show me that in order to be a good problem solver, we have to think outside of the box that we place ourselves in and be willing to negotiate outside of our own team. There are so many resource channels that we can open ourselves up to by building our networks and thinking outside of the limitations on our own teams.

There are three simple steps to effective negotiation. Although fourth graders could not put it into these words, they taught me through their actions, with the "Building Bridges" activity, that these steps provide the best opportunity for successful negotiation.

Define your Objective

How can we possibly expect to be a good negotiator if we don't know exactly what we want out of the negotiation? We must know what we want as well as defining our best and worst case scenarios. If we are willing to accept less than what we are asking for, we need to know it up front. We need to distinguish between what we need and what we want and what value we place on those needs and wants. "I knew exactly what we needed, we needed tape, bad! And quick, before my team continued to yell at me," Samantha explained as she finished the negotiation during the "Building Bridges" activity.

Understand the Objective of the Other Party

This can be even more important than knowing what you want or need. Know what the other person wants and understand how you can help that person get what they want. Go into the negotiation understanding the needs of the other party and how you can meet those needs. Dad was right, "Help someone get what they want and you will be able to get what you want."

By understanding what roles you can play in helping someone accomplish their objective, you will be that much more successful in any negotiation. It's like Bobby, age eleven explained to me after class. "I'm in a fantasy baseball league. I tried to trade Pedro Martinez for Manny Ramirez. It's a fair trade. In fact, I think I'm giving up even more. But he didn't need a pitcher; he only really needed a catcher. Once I saw that, I offered him a catcher, hoping to get Manny Ramirez. It worked! ... even though I think he should've taken Pedro!"

Propose a Solution

Once we understand what we need and what the other person or team needs, we can then begin to process potential solutions. Too often, we try to come up with the solution before we really understand what the other person needs or wants. We think we are offering a fair trade, but in reality, it doesn't meet the needs of the other person and we simply won't be successful in our negotiation that way. It's important to firm up our understanding of each party's needs before drawing up solutions, particularly in negotiations that involve more than two parties. Samantha said, "As soon as I saw that they needed newspaper, I saw an opportunity to negotiate with them. They had a need that we could fill; we had a need that they could fill. The solution came pretty easy after that."

Without a doubt, there are countless other variables that are important for effective negotiation. There have been volumes and volumes written on effective negotiation, such as how to give yourself the upper hand in a negotiation. Some of the variables that play an important role in negotiation include both verbal and nonverbal communication, strategy, timing, proposal presentation and inarguably, lots more. Ten and eleven year-old children taught me the basic building blocks of successful negotiations: understand what you want, what the other person wants, and then think about solving the problem. I think about how I negotiate everyday and so often I'm already thinking about what kind of proposal I can make in the negotiation, without really understanding what the other person wants or needs. Then I think about those two scientists with the oranges. If only I had known that my partner only needed the peelings!

CONCLUSION

PUTTING THE PUZZLE PIECES TOGETHER

Take a few minutes and try to define the word team. Many people would describe the word "team" as a group of people who work together to accomplish a task. It is amazing how many people use the words group and team interchangeably, when in fact they are very different. The Merriam-Webster dictionary defines a team as "a number of persons associated together in work or activity." With all due respect to Merriam-Webster, fourth and fifth graders have come up with far better definitions:

"A team is more than a group. A team is well-organized, and trusts each other. A team gets more done because we work together," said, Amanda age ten.

"A team works hard together and supports each other. I think a team feeds off each other," added Sean, age twelve.

"You can't form a team. You can form a group. And slowly a group becomes a team by using these skills, like strategizing," stated Craig, age ten.

"A team works as one." Miranda, age eleven.

Arriving at an appropriate definition for teamwork is far from the end objective, far from the goal of managers trying to develop teamwork in their workplace and far from the goals of the 2+2=5 program. We must move from words to actions. This can be done by focusing on the team and interpersonal skills and exercising those skills over time through developmental activities. Managers

CONCLUSION

must leverage opportunities to hone and develop these skills in their employees. These skills extend farther than in the workplace. In addition, families must apply these skills to tighten the family team unit.

Each skill that the 2+2=5 program focuses on: leadership, communication, problem solving, negotiation, diversity, and trust are all essential to the development of high-performing teams. Each team that ever went through the 2+2=5 program demonstrated that don't have at least a little bit of each of these integral team skills and the team must have a mix of skills and talents. For example, you simply can't have a team of individuals who insist on being the leader and get caught in a whirlwind of power struggle. Teams must find a mix and balance of these skills in order to be successful.

Laura, a fifth grade student, had the last word when she said, "Teamwork is important everyday, in everything we do. Two plus two really can equal five, but we have to work at it!"